Contents

Leading from the Trenches

What It Takes to Become an Instructional Leader

Stephen V. Newton

ROWMAN & LITTLEFIELD
Lanham • Boulder • New York • London

Published by Rowman & Littlefield
An imprint of The Rowman & Littlefield Publishing Group, Inc.
4501 Forbes Boulevard, Suite 200, Lanham, Maryland 20706
www.rowman.com

Unit A, Whitacre Mews, 26–34 Stannary Street, London SE11 4AB

British Library Cataloguing in Publication Information Available

Library of Congress Cataloging-in-Publication Data Available

ISBN (cloth : alk. paper) 978-1-4758-4374-3
ISBN (paper : alk. paper) 978-1-4758-4375-0
ISBN (electronic) 978-1-4758-4376-7

♾™ The paper used in this publication meets the minimum requirements of American National Standard for Information Sciences—Permanence of Paper for Printed Library Materials, ANSI/NISO Z39.48–1992.

Printed in the United States of America

Preface

The origin of this book is rooted in my own professional struggles. Early in my administrative career, I had the good fortune of being surrounded by colleagues who were able to give me critical feedback in ways that did not cause me to shut down but rather opened my eyes to my own limitations and failings.

In my preparatory work to become a school principal, I completed a master's degree in educational administration. This coursework was focused on broad topics that were certainly functions of the principalship. Learning about budgets, teacher evaluations, and school law certainly served me well as I made the transition from the classroom into the principal's office.

However, I knew I had major gaps in my ability to lead. After three years as a principal, I began to consider getting a doctorate in education. As I looked at those around me pursuing their education, all of my peers seemed to continue educational leadership studies into their next degree.

After several conversations with teachers who were asking me very difficult questions about my opinion on serious instructional issues, I had a moment of clarity. I realized that I was learning how to lead others. I was fair and consistent. I was rational and thoughtful in my dealings with others. But as strong as I felt in knowing *how* to lead, I wondered if I knew *what* to lead.

I then enrolled in a doctoral program in curriculum and instruction with a focus on secondary literacy. My professional studies took on a strong emphasis in developing credibility in the work of the classroom. As a result, I believe I created a link between the world of instruction and leadership.

In my subsequent years working with both teachers and principals, I sense that the gap is widening. Both teachers and principals are being asked to do more and more, but there seems to be less common ground than ever before.

The purpose of this book is to create a collaborative space between teachers and administrators. Principals must take the lead in this conversation as it is contrary to the role of the teacher to find that common ground in an administrative office.

The most powerful and genuine space for the meeting of these two groups of professionals is in the classroom. It is in the classroom that the most consequential and powerful work happens. Principals cannot fail to grasp the importance of finding their voice within the heart of their own school.

This book is my attempt to create a professional bridge between teachers and principals that will result in work of great consequence. This work is possible and is critical if we are committed to improving the lives of students. This work is not for the timid. This work will stretch the skills and commitment of the principal, but it is worth it.

This work cannot be done at a distance. This work requires that everyone involved get dirty hands. The principal must get in the trenches with teachers. It is from this strategic point in the trenches that the principal must lead.

Acknowledgments

This book is a compilation of the experiences, opportunities, and relationships that I have been blessed with in this world. In particular, I would like to thank a number of people for their help and support in making this book a reality.

To my wife, Amanda, thank you for your love and support in everything I do.

To my children, Alexandra, Mackenzie, Hunter, Colin, Ava, and Elise, thank you for your encouragement and patience with your distracted father.

To Dr. Tom Koerner, thank you for believing in this idea from the very beginning before a single word had been written.

To Kelly Mihalik, thank you for your constant encouragement and advice in the writing and editing of this manuscript.

To Emily Tuttle and all of the fine people at Rowman & Littlefield, thank you for investing your professional time and expertise in producing this book.

Introduction

Someone will lead. Someone always does. At all times, someone is leading the people in every organization. But, is the one currently leading doing the right things for the right fundamental purpose? Unfortunately, this is not always the case. Leaders are supposed to help others find their way. Oftentimes, the leader who emerges is simply not the right person.

It is a colossal mistake to assume that the person at the highest pay grade who has been entrusted with the keys to the front doors is the person leading in the organization. It is also a mistake to assume that the one leading has been designated to do so. It is a mistake to assume that schools are rudderless if the principal is not functioning as a leader. This is never the case. Someone is leading. Someone is always leading. Unfortunately, the one leading may be leading others into chaos and disarray.

What portion of the world has been entrusted to your care? Who is currently leading them? Administrators must assess who is in control of their building and regain that control if it is not them. Some may need to regain it by re-establishing their own place as leader, removing the inappropriate adoption of power that others have attained. Some may need to reawaken their own sense of obligation to lead in the ways they should.

As leaders help others find their way, it is often in a collaborative manner, bringing everyone together to reach a goal for a common purpose. However, it is more nuanced than that. While a group may share a common purpose, the role that each plays in that goal can be vastly different. Leadership is not exercised by getting everyone to do the same thing. True leadership is discerning the role that each person is capable of playing and assisting them in maximizing that potential within themselves. It is a constant and responsive act in illuminating and assisting just enough that the

1

others find new and better ways to do what they are asked to do. This is in stark contrast to the traditional vision of one strong leader with submissive and devoted followers lining up to do as they are told. True leaders assist others in finding their own way, developing them into leaders themselves on the journey.

Chapter 1

Surveying the Landscape

A special call for leadership has been placed upon the shoulders of school leaders. Leaders in education play a unique role, different from leaders in any other profession. To begin to understand what it means to be an excellent leader of a school, it is important to understand the intricacies of the school environment. The current landscape in education is a result of an evolution in expectations placed on schools and their leaders. Administrators have seen a drastic transformation in the context and expectations that have been leveled upon schools in the past few decades. In this new setting, leaders must adapt to the needs of the teachers and children entrusted to their care.

The context in which schools exist today has radically changed over the years. In addition to traditional expectations placed on educators, schools are now required to address both academic and new societal obligations that formerly did not exist. This nonexhaustive list includes drug and alcohol abuse, bullying, suicide awareness, cyber safety, pregnancy awareness, character education, and dropout prevention. Each of these serious topics demands great care and attention to ensure students are safe, and each of these societal issues has, in large part, been placed upon schools to address. No longer is the teacher able to be a master of content alone. Rather, a teacher must be an expert at algebra and recognizing the signs of teen depression. This is a daunting task for anyone. While it could be argued whether kids are different today, it is irrefutable that the societal context in which kids exist has never before been as it is today.

Not only are schools faced with the distraction of teaching many topics that were far beyond the original mission of schools, but also students themselves are faced with for more distracting and debilitating issues than ever before. For example, the sheer number of available and possible drugs to abuse has skyrocketed in a generation. Every social ill has flourished in quantity and

3

variety and has ventured into mainstream America. Quite simply, there are far more things that kids must refuse. As beneficial as instantaneous Internet access is, this perpetual connectivity has created perpetual distraction. Of course, this phenomenon is exacerbated in young people who physiologically are battling impulse control at all times. Aside from the distractions of our modern times, it is, quite honestly, much more dangerous to be a young person in our schools today. A generation ago, students worried about potential nuclear conflicts thousands of miles away. The child today wonders if the next school shooting will hit close to home. Yet, in the midst of all of this, the time-honored task of educating children must continue.

In recent years, much attention has been focused on dropout prevention and on-time graduation rate. This is certainly a noble task, and many educators are devoting their professional lives to pulling students back from the ledge, going so far as to knock on trailer house doors to convince students to give school another try. There is no doubt that these efforts are paying dividends, and many students are re-enrolling and graduating. Without the intervention of caring educators, these students would have simply faded into the dark corners of our communities, piecing together low-skilled jobs, if any at all. A generation ago, this was the reality for marginalized students. When they left school, it was rare if anyone went looking for them.

In response to more students re-enrolling in schools, educators are faced with the daunting task of reassimilating these students into the classroom. More than one educator have concluded that schools are literally teaching a kind of student who never persisted in classrooms previously. Of course, this is coupled together with the added challenge and burden of increasingly rigorous graduation requirements. It was not unheard of a generation ago for schools to require only two years of mathematics to graduate. These requirements often required that the lowest-performing students complete a course in algebra and geometry. Now, it is commonplace for all students, regardless of performance level or underlying disability, to complete four years of mathematics, including college-preparatory algebra II. Educators must teach every discipline they have ever taught, often with more rigorous demands, to students who are more distracted than ever before while sitting next to a group of kids who are more at-risk than ever. It is no wonder that veteran teachers often conclude that they are not in the same business that they were thirty years ago.

As the educational landscape shifted, so too did the opinion of the public regarding the attitudes and expectations of educators. Unfortunately, public education has been politicized on both sides of the political aisle in aggressive ways. With both sides attempting to cherry-pick facts and figures to support their given agenda, schools are left to feel as if they are not getting the job done adequately while working harder than ever.

In an effort to be all things to everyone, no one seems satisfied. Schools are criticized by all for failing to focus exclusively on the needs of a variety of squeaky wheels. Sides are being drawn to advocate for a myriad of causes while children and the adults committed to helping them are caught in the crossfire. Often, educators are torn between competing interests within the same child. Parents want their children to have a high-quality college-preparatory experience but become furious if their student receives anything less than an A in all classes. Like never before, the principalship demands a special sort of courage and vision not only to restore the public confidence but also to lead the students in our community to become leaders in a competitive global economy. Schools must prepare students to contribute immediately to the very society that is skeptical about their worth.

Education has become a battlefield. Caught in the crossfire of this battlefield are the children of this nation. Children desperately need help and will not likely get their needs met unless it is by the teachers who are committed to them. In an age when the stabilizing forces of historical institutions such as churches and extended families have diminished greatly in the lives of many children, the public school stands in the breech to assist where others are not. Public schools have become the last line of defense for many, and a source of tremendous support and reliance for most.

Some may conclude that it is a bit overdramatic to describe the public school as the last bastion of hope for kids but make that argument to a student who eats all three meals inside the four walls of the school and who dreads the prospect of staying home for a three-day weekend. It can be easy to forget that this is the reality for many because it is not the reality for all.

Educating a classroom of students is a daunting task, even if the duties are stripped down to the bare minimum of teaching course content. Millions of teachers each day face nearly insurmountable odds, picking themselves and their students up, taking on the most difficult challenges. The school leader must recognize what the students in the building need and bring staff together to successfully perform the hard work of meeting those needs. This critical work cannot be left to chance. Like hot coals in a campfire, heat is sustained and generated when the fuel is near to another. However, when a coal is separated from the heap, it soon cools and no longer serves its primary purpose until the tender of the fire reforms the coals into a pile. This is the role of the school leader. Relying upon strong, purposeful systems that bring people together around a common purpose is the only way to produce a powerful effect. When teachers stray too far away from a united purpose, whether intentional or not, the fervor and effect of their purpose cool and diminish quickly. A strong leader gathers the hot coals of passionate teachers together to keep them focused on the kinds of work that will be of the most consequence.

Historically, the principal of a school has often been relegated to the role of manager: monitoring recess, building a master schedule, and supervising an athletic event. While the bulk of this principal's day is focused on a stream of managerial tasks, the teachers work as independent contractors, loosely held together by a common parking lot. When teachers are allowed to function in isolation with little quality control, a manager seems to be just what the system needs. Someone who is able to create just enough ties to hold the system together while the pieces function independently suffices under these circumstances. A school manager makes sure that the parts are well oiled and nothing interferes with the work of independent contractors.

This view of a school administrator is a sad departure from the origin of the role. Of course, originally schools were led by a *principal teacher*, or *principal* for short. In these times, the role of teacher was inextricably bound in the identity of the principal. Somewhere along the line, this was lost.

The schools of today are demanding far more from leaders than managing the building. There is certainly a vast difference between creating a lunch schedule and ensuring students are college and career-ready to function in a global society. The latter demands far more than moving the right pieces on the board to the best places. School leadership focused on maximizing student achievement requires more, better, and different things from both the adults and students in schools. These new efforts require intentional action on the part of strong leaders for successful implementation.

Leadership now demands an intimate knowledge and understanding of student academic abilities. This requires leaders to be connected with the operation of classrooms in a new way. Perhaps in the past, administrators had the luxury of touching base with teachers for status reports and updates on a periodic basis. In that world, as long as the teacher had not violated school policy, the outcomes for kids were completely within the control of the teacher. With this approach, the chips just fell where they may with levels of student achievement depend upon the interest, commitment, and skill level of teachers.

A new approach to educational leadership does not discount the importance of teachers or their decision-making abilities. However, it does demand a broader inclusion of input in decision making from other stakeholders. Schools must now offer *multiple* second chances to assist students in finding success. While good-hearted teachers have often worked to extend extra help to their students, the new expectation is that schools, led by the principal, weave these practices into the very fabric of their operation rather than leaving them to the discretion of willing teachers only. This demands not only active leadership in oversight of classroom practices but also deep involvement to move and evolve the entire system to embrace better practices.

These skills have not always been historically prized or required within the principalship. Now, they are integral in a healthy educational system. The first step for a principal is to recognize that the emerging needs of students have rewritten the job description. This can be daunting to a leader who has built a successful career without these demands in mind. Further, part of the reason many educational systems are floundering is because some leaders are indeed continuing to function as managers despite the new demands. Parents are simply unaware of how their principal should be engaging in the instructional conversation because their child's principal is functioning much like the principal they had in their own youth. Why might they expect anything different if they have never experienced it? This is tragic for students trapped in this environment. The students' best chance at an exemplary educational experience is in the hands of a leader who has not chosen nor has been forced into best instructional practices. Educational leaders must have the courage to look beyond their current job description and expectations and make new decisions on what their role should be. Public schools are facing very unique challenges. These challenges demand a new and special kind of leadership.

When a school leader embraces this call to leadership, it remains critically important to remember that leadership does not happen within a vacuum. Leadership is very much a social activity. It involves others and affects others. Leaders must be fully cognizant of who is touched by their new efforts. While the outcome of the work is to the benefit of children and their families, the heavy lifting required is borne upon the backs of a principal's work with teachers.

Current theories on leadership often begin with the advice to "get the right people on the bus." When authors talk about getting the right people on the bus, they are often speaking to an audience in the private sector. Most businesses have a clearly defined metric to demonstrate success or failure. Corporate leaders have made great waves in discussing their approach to firing their lowest performers by sharply focused efforts to discern high performers from their lower-functioning counterparts.

A business can control the quality of its raw materials and all aspects of production. It can then measure results with hard numbers while tightly controlling all variables. Education, on the other hand, has no control of its raw materials. Education differs in a fundamental way in this regard. Leaders in education must strive to coach teachers to achieve excellence as opposed to simply eliminating those who aren't presently meeting expectations. To fire teachers indiscriminately would suggest that they are in control of enough variables to reliably predict the outcome. Parents send the best kids they have. Some of these kids are prepared to learn; others are not. Some are well fed; others are not. Some value the very education they are receiving;

others do not. This is a fundamental difference between education and the business world.

Further, leaders cannot control all aspects of their professional environment. Imagine the chaos that would ensue upon the production floor of a car manufacturer if people snuck in the back door and sabotaged the equipment on a regular basis. Schools have very little ability to control the outside forces and detrimental influences that impact a child's ability to learn. What schools can control is the actions of educators during the time kids are present within the school year.

Because the metric of success is difficult to measure and assign credit (how much of a student's success on an exam is due to the teacher compared to good study habits, parental involvement, and preparation received in prior years?), it is very difficult for school leaders to reach inarguable conclusions about a teacher's performance. While principals certainly have strong opinions on which teachers are effective and which ones are not, the water is often sufficiently muddy that reaching a defendable conclusion about teacher performance is difficult. The difficulty that principals have in removing weak teachers across this nation is simply not due to a lack of will or interest of principals in having the best teachers in front of their students. Instead, principals are often forced to accept some professionals on their bus whom they'd prefer not to let on board given their druthers.

Leaders must quickly come to the realization that they will likely have very little control over who they will be leading. Of course there is an exception if somebody violates the law or ethical practices. However, most likely, the principal will have to make do with existing staff rather than bringing onboard new faculty members.

While this may be a sobering reality, it is not necessarily a bad place to begin. If teachers in the existing system are not operating in optimal ways, it may be largely due to poor leadership in prior years. The bright spot in this scenario is that the existing personnel are familiar with the clientele in the current environment. Many human resources officials will readily admit that it is easier and more cost-effective to retrain existing staff rather than trying to train new hires.

Of course, periodically a principal will have the opportunity to hire new staff. Leaders must recognize the tremendous gift that this provides and take great pains to hire somebody who understands and is willing to commit to the new vision of leadership in the building. Great grains in progress can be made with existing staff and that should not be overlooked or given as a reason for failure to improve conditions.

Principals must take great care in getting to know and objectively evaluating those who are on the bus. This requires more thoughtful effort than reviewing former evaluations or listening to casual opinions offered by opinionated staff members. In reality, the principal must conduct a very thorough audit and analysis of the people who are teaching, their particular strengths and weaknesses, and their likely potential to improve. Assessing potential to improve is a critically important function at this juncture. Teachers are often only as good as they are asked to be, and many are quite capable of performing at much higher levels of performance if they are shown the way.

With even a cursory review of any staff, principals will quickly realize that they are dealing with a diverse group of individuals. It is important to note that people have a tendency to pigeonhole others and describe them in ways that do not take their full complexity into account. Often, a prevailing personal characteristic or a specific scenario causes a leader to mentally categorize a teacher. For example, a principal may not think much further than the memory of a teacher yelling at a parent in a contentious meeting. That memory may come to represent and dominate all thoughts about the teacher.

These incomplete characterizations of others may be a decent starting point, but then substantial thought and reflection is required moving forward. People are complex. Each person acts in certain ways depending upon the social situations and may act quite differently in a different time and space. While people may be somewhat predictable in a given situation, the environment a person is in may determine whether he or she acts assertively or passively. This phenomenon is true for everyone. It is important to note that the principal is likely to see and deal with people in a very narrow band of circumstances. The way in which teachers behave in a faculty meeting is likely to be very different from the way they conduct themselves in a classroom setting. Imagine the incorrect assumptions could be made if the principal rarely walked into classroom to see the various skill sets and personality traits that emerge in a different environment.

It is also important to note that even if the principal has observed a teacher in the classroom, it has been under the conditions where a teacher is trying to function naturally with a supervisor standing a few feet away observing every move. If this relationship is not well established and comfortable, even a firsthand observation of a teacher in action could likely be very different from normal behavior. Nature enthusiasts are quick to remember that when an animal notices the observer, it is no longer a natural environment.

Principals are often confronted with the phenomenon that some coworkers are good teachers, some are good colleagues, some are both, and some are neither. This presents an interesting dilemma and a potential trap for principals. For example, suppose a principal were to engage in an exercise determining the potential of a staff member and recalls that the teacher in question is very popular with kids. This is the teacher that chaperones all of the dances, has students who want to hang out in the classroom after school, and is the coach for the cheerleading team.

Further, the teacher has worked there for a decade and has never sent a student to the office, is the principal's biggest fan for new ideas, and is very pleasant and engaging in conversation each morning before school. This paints a pretty compelling picture of a person good to kids and easy to work around. But, suppose that the principal walks by the classroom each day and notices the kids thoroughly enjoying themselves but minimally engaged in productive academic work. What should a principal make of this? This may be a professional who is a good colleague but a subpar teacher.

Conversely, it is easy to imagine a teacher who continually complains to the principal about working conditions, challenges the principal during faculty meetings about planned innovations, and is a bit grumpy upon arrival each morning. This does not paint a very good picture for this teacher being a valued colleague. However, what should a principal conclude if he or she walks by this teacher's classroom and sees thirty kids diligently engaged in meaningful instruction and lively discussion with this teacher? Might this be a lousy colleague but a dynamic teacher?

Likely, the principal might find it difficult to be too hard on the first teacher. The teacher probably gets a pass on a day-to-day basis by being such a pleasant colleague. The principal may grin and bear it knowing that there is not a lot of learning happening in the classroom. Perhaps the principal even concludes that it is probably okay because the affective component to education is important and often neglected in the lives of kids. This teacher, after all, may be the one bright spot in some of these kids' lives. Perhaps the principal is unable to hear the quiet voice in her head reminding her that excellent teachers take good care of students *and* teach them important things. The principal in this scenario, though, is torn. Of all the battles that must be fought in education, is it really worth picking a fight with the most popular and pleasant person in the school?

Similarly, the principal probably groans and rolls her eyes when the second teacher approaches. What is it going to be this time? The teacher constantly second-guesses all decisions and seems to undermine the principal's authority by asking professionally embarrassing questions in an open forum. Does this principal find it hard to believe that this teacher is capable of powerful work in the classroom? One can imagine how poorly the principal might consider this teacher if the principal never observed the teacher in action to see genuine effective practices.

If the principal in this scenario were assembling a building leadership team to talk about needed improvements within the school, which teacher is she most likely to select? Obviously, the principal would prefer to pass the time in committee meetings with the pleasant colleague. This teacher would likely be easy to work with within the leadership team setting but may be offering suggestions for improvement while being completely unaware of best instructional practices.

Thus, the principal can easily slip into dangerous territory. After all, what is gained if honest attempts to grow leaders and improve practice are stunted by the principal's inability to recognize talent within the staff? The entire credibility of improvement efforts are at stake if a faculty quietly recognizes that the wrong people have been assembled for the wrong reasons trying to engage in the right work.

Principals must not only survey the landscape of their teachers' individual strengths and weaknesses but also measure those against a realistic and genuine appraisal of where the school currently functions academically. A firm understanding of the current academic reality is the only logical starting point to begin mapping out another destination. The leader must have the right goal but also execute a sensible plan to reach that goal. If the goal is to arrive at a distant point by the end of the school year, it logically follows that some portion of that distance is gained each and every day. Often, leaders have good and noble goals but rather lousy plans. It is easy to get caught up in thinking and talking about the ultimate destination. Sometimes, this is because it provides a convenient distraction from focusing on the day's work at hand. Once a goal is established, principals must consider the current landscape that surrounds them and the personnel who will be doing the work and decide upon what portion of work can be done at this moment.

After taking a comprehensive assessment of the existing state of the school—the students and their needs, the teachers and their skill sets, the culture, and the community—it is time to take a look at school improvement. What specific changes must be made to improve the landscape? What resources will be necessary? Who can help with these change efforts? These are the questions that will help guide the work that needs to be done to transition the current landscape into an environment that develops skillful teachers and successful students. Change will be necessary to grow and improve as professionals and as a school building. It may take some convincing to move others to adopt new practices that will bring about better results for students.

Educators often beat themselves up for the amount of work that is not possible at any given moment. This is an important reality that must be acknowledged. Nobody can do everything they wish to do at any given time. Plans unfold in a social context. Some things the team is ready for and other things are simply not possible. The trick is to ensure that the work that a leader believes is not yet possible is in fact accurate and is not just reaching that conclusion because the next portion of work to be done is going to be difficult and challenging. This can be best accomplished by focusing the work within the moment. What can be done today? Perhaps a school is not yet ready to adopt a wide-scale reform effort, but certain individuals are already engaging in those efforts, and work could be done to recruit other willing participants to join them. Assessing the capacity to embrace new work among teachers is critical before beginning any new endeavor.

It is also important to consider the professional will and capacity of a school principal's supervisors. Are the district-level supervisors ready and willing to support new efforts? Principals must not only engage in this type of reflective questioning about the support from a supervisor but also ask what indicators could be relied upon to accurately estimate the support they are likely to receive.

One way to approach this delicate task is to engage in a frank conversation with supervisors about the proposed plans and likely resistance that will follow. It is important that this conversation does not create a climate of fear where it becomes easier to shut down the proposed work. Rather, it must be a candid conversation that honestly describes the specific people and groups who may resist the change. This should be balanced by a discussion of the other groups who are already engaging in the work (or are at least interested in pursuing it). This paints a landscape where everyone involved in supporting the work has a true understanding of the opposition but also has an understanding that good people will be frustrated if the work is not supported.

Further, a leader would be wise to paint a very clear picture about the ways in which this new work will create new and better opportunities for students. It becomes much easier to withstand criticism of some laggards if it is balanced by strong educators, supportive parents, and the best interests of children.

Leaders must bring their supervisors to a crossroads and be as specific as:

> Our achievement data show that students are struggling in mathematics. I believe our next step needs to be the creation of a tutorial period at the end of the school day. Mrs. Kelly and Mr. Rogers have already begun to conduct sessions informally on their own, but their rooms simply cannot contain all of the students that need help. If we were to require all math teachers to dedicate thirty minutes after school to this new program, I am sure Mr. Turner will object and claim it is another class he is being forced to teach and is not being financially compensated to do so. I can also imagine that the basketball coach will be upset that his players cannot get to practice as quickly. We are at a crossroads. This is a new idea that was wildly supported by our recent parent survey. It will give students more one on one time with their math instructor, but you may hear a few objections. Can you support this new requirement in my school?

This scenario paints a balanced picture of what is proposed, why it supports good practice, and the realities of those in opposition to the work. It is foolish for leaders to attempt to implement change that will be immediately scuttled by their superiors. It is even more foolish to keep the superiors in the dark about important developments and hope that they are supportive after the work begins and the opposition then becomes vocal. Leaders must recognize that in these conversations, there are tremendous opportunities to lead and influence their superiors as well.

A superior hires a school-level leader with the express intention that he or she will tend to the direction of the building. Many superintendents are waiting and willing to be led by building-level principals who have insight on the next, most appropriate steps for the building to take. Principals often forget that their leadership obligations do not only run downhill. Superiors cannot be caught up in the details of the building. That is simply not their job. That does not mean, however, that they do not care about the building. Rather, they are (hopefully) wise enough to allow the building principal to function as a leader, exerting support when it is necessary. Principals who do not take the time to lead their superiors in matters that have been entrusted to them are missing out on the breadth that true leadership requires.

So much has been written about implementing change across systems that an entire discipline of change theory has emerged in the literature base. There is no doubt that change can be incredibly difficult at times. One must only look at a person who takes smoking breaks while being administered oxygen to know that it is often difficult to change even in the midst of dire circumstances.

However, it ought to be noted that not all change should be seen as this difficult. Indeed, some change is immediately welcomed and incorporated into daily life without much thought. For example, if someone were to hand out everyone's favorite coffee upon arrival at work each day, this sort of change would be immediately welcomed. This generosity would not need to be slowly processed or acclimated to over time. In fact, receiving a free coffee each day would be so easily welcomed that a person may begin to expect it and even feel entitled to it in a short amount of time.

Change is not always hard. Therefore, it is important for a leader to remember objecting to a proposed change should not be the immediate reaction at all times. Nor should a leader indulge some people's tendency to invoke the inherent difficulties of change at every twist and turn professionally. It is wrong to invoke the nuances of change theory, for example, if a principal makes a simple change to the lunch schedule. Invoking the challenges of change at the wrong time diminishes the difficulty that some change does indeed present. Some change is hard; other change should not be.

Education is certainly rife with change. Some of the efforts are as simple as changing the lunch schedule, but others are, in fact, difficult to process and find ways to adapt. Leaders should take great care to make sure that teachers receive the proper training and resources to ensure that the change effort is likely to succeed. Beyond that, much of the resistance to change and use of change theory as an excuse can be more readily dismissed than some in the change theory community might suggest. The problem with invoking change theory is that it often leaves people paralyzed in the intersection.

For example, if the principal in the previous example decided to implement the proposed math tutorial time that was discussed with the superintendent, one might imagine a number of staff members finding the new work to be a difficult change to add into their busy day. Indeed, some may offer reasons why it won't work:

"The kids won't even come."
"There will be too many kids to give anyone any meaningful help."
"I don't know how I'm supposed to jump from algebra with one student to geometry with another."

The list could go on and on. Some may even invoke some of the tenets of change theory in their objections:

"Change like this takes time."
"Maybe we should conduct a survey to see if it is even needed."
"We are overwhelmed already. You keep putting things on our plate but never take anything off."

What exactly is a principal to make of responses like these? This first thing that must happen is that the leader must recall why the change effort was being proposed in the first place. The answer, of course, is that large numbers of students were failing miserably in math. What was being done in response to it? Nothing. Plain and simple. The best and genuine efforts of hardworking math teachers aside, kids are struggling. Within that present state of struggle, nothing new was happening.

The principal is now in an intersection. Dangers are pressing in from all four sides, and there is an outcry to do nothing. Stay motionless in the intersection because change for the grownups is hard. It is important to remember that it really is not the principal or the teachers in this dangerous intersection. It is the children. If educators realize that students are in academic jeopardy, something new must be done. Try something. Anything. But do not remain paralyzed in the intersection. This seems to be an unintended consequence of those who mistakenly invoke change theory as a rationale for inaction.

Proponents of change theory may rightfully object that this criticism is not the intended result of appreciating the complexities of enacting change. Fair enough. However, it is important to examine the historic tendencies in education when powerful and consequential initiatives are recommended.

For example, in spite of numerous studies citing the immediate and powerful academic achievements associated with the use of formative assessments, many classrooms in this country make little use of formative assessment on a daily basis. Principals and teacher leaders have been advocating for the implementation of these practices in a systemic way at least since Benjamin Bloom's description in 1971. The first students who benefited from the distinction between formative and summative assessments are now teachers themselves in the twilight of their own teaching careers. Yet, in most schools, there are at least a few teachers who continue to neglect this important practice. Some may argue that change takes time. For those keeping score at home, this change has taken several decades to get through the intersection. Most educators could probably reflect on the efforts in their own district that were initiated five, ten, even fifteen years ago that are not being implemented fully. Without exception, there are always those lagging behind admonishing everybody else that change takes time.

Likely, this has not gone unnoticed by good-hearted principals seeking to accomplish important work. Perhaps they are wondering how to move others through the intersection. Reflecting upon examples throughout life where significant change actually occurred provides important lessons in this regard. For every person who struggles to kick a cigarette habit, there are others who quit cold turkey. For every person who is paralyzed professionally and unwilling to evolve with their industry, there are others who reinvent themselves professionally after twenty years on the job. The addicted become clean; the lazy become hard workers; the mean-spirited become gentle-hearted toward others. It is easy to focus on those who persist in their inability and unwillingness to change. But what about those others who defy the odds and do change?

There is an underlying theme that transcends drug addiction, professional risk taking, and all other brave souls turning over new leaves in life. The common thread that runs through all of these fundamental changes is that these people find a way to focus on something greater than themselves. Both Maslow and common sense argue that human beings demand specific basic needs in order to survive. Along with food, water, and shelter, people also have a need for a sense of security. Beyond this, humans can begin the process of self-actualization. While that may seem to be a lofty goal only achieved by a few, in reality, most people are somewhere along the spectrum of fulfilling their dreams and aspirations. However, it does appear that some people, especially those who are confronted with change, tend to falter in properly defining their own sense of security.

Much like a small child claiming to be starving when they are simply hungry for the next meal, some people often *overreact* to the stress of implementing new change in their professional lives. In these moments, many would suggest that their very security is at stake. Leaders owe it to their followers to frame properly what is being asked of them and how the new work may indeed challenge their current skill set, but it is far from threatening their well-being.

As one progresses up the pyramid of needs, it is clear that the most basic needs are very personal ones. After those are secure, a person is better able to focus on someone other than themselves. All people instinctively become selfish to ensure that their most basic needs are being met. This is not only universal, but it makes perfect sense as well. But what happens when people falsely believe their sense of security is being threatened? Perhaps these people need to be nudged into realizing their fears are more shadow than real. This does not dismiss true threats but forces people to recognize the true challenge in front of them for what it truly is.

When a leader is able to reframe the fear of change that people feel and assist them in recognizing that it is new but not necessarily threatening, teachers can begin to process the work for what it truly is. This is also the moment the leader needs to be firm with those who wish to frame new professional work as a true threat to their basic needs. These are not easy conversations but are entirely necessary. People need to recognize the moments where they are called to serve others and are completely capable of doing so, but instead turn inward and think more about their own perceived needs than the needs of those who they have been charged to assist.

In these moments, a leader must keep firm pressure upon those in the conversation to frame the underlying purpose of the new work. There is no doubt that the adults in the system will be the ones doing the work. Those resisting change never forget that they are the ones engaged in difficult work. The problem is that is where they desire to keep the focus. However, the leader must persist in the conversation to remind others that the new work is for the benefit of children. Often, people must be forced out of their own inward focus and refocus in an outward fashion on those who they have been both hired and called to serve.

A leader must paint a very clear and descriptive picture of the present state of need and the urgency behind the new work. If a leader cannot express an urgency to the change effort, it is probably a fair question whether the change effort is indeed necessary. Supposing that the improvement effort is indeed beneficial for students, the principal must paint a dramatic vision of the present state of need and how the teachers' efforts will remedy the problem.

Focusing on something greater than themselves is not only a way to bring individuals along in the change effort, but it is also a powerful way to get diverse groups of adults working together collaboratively. Simply, the work must be about others beyond the individual team members or even the team dynamic itself. Everyone must be reminded whom they are serving. It is in these moments that principals are often painfully reminded that there are some in the profession who do indeed work *with* kids but are often reluctant to work *for* kids.

This is where the true line in the sand in education must be drawn. It is not a line to be drawn determining who should be fired. That is far too simplistic and does not solve the underlying problem. It is a line where professionals truly discuss the lengths they intend to go to help children. This is quite different from the tendency most educators have in saying that any given idea should be supported because it is "good for kids." Rather it is an honest and descriptive conversation about what needs to be done for young people and how adults intend to do it despite resistance and obstacles. Indeed, it even requires a discussion of the internal resistance that is keeping the work from getting done. This is possible only if a leader sharply focuses the conversation on what is at stake for kids. It is critical to remember and remind all involved that young people will continue to bear the burden until the adults get their act together and make necessary changes. For young people, the stakes are extremely high and time is short.

If kids were not suffering in so many different ways, such dramatic terms may not be necessary. However, that is simply not the case. While many problems are not initiated within the school system, educators are often able to provide relief from them by their actions. These societal ills are not the fault of educators, but they are the educators' problems. While many of the problems are inconceivably deep and persistent, many others are quite possible to address in meaningful ways. Simply, educators do not have to worry about fixing the most difficult problems yet because many challenges with easy answers that others have already solved are not being addressed. With nearly every challenge in front of educators, somebody somewhere has found success. That person's work must be replicated.

Of course, many would suggest that their current reality is different somehow from the situation other people are encountering. Somehow, the line of reasoning is that the success others may be seeing does not translate to a possibility in the naysayer's school. Their reality is different. For the school that cannot solve challenging problems, it makes good sense. It is too painful to admit that educators in another place are producing better results. This attitude needs to be confronted immediately and often. It is not easier to be a homeless student on one side of town than another. Likewise, algebra is not easier to learn in Philadelphia than Chicago.

Many educators have created complex narratives to justify and explain why their set of challenges have never been seen before and are likely insolvable for reasons that other schools couldn't possibly understand. Ironically, the school down the street is likely constructing the same faulty narrative to excuse its own struggles. Whatever the reason adults suggest for this underperformance, it comes at a very dangerous price. Bound up deeply within this narrative is the assertion that kids are inherently damaged. If a set of challenges are truly unique, it could only be because the children in that setting are fundamentally inferior.

This attitude cannot help but shape the way in which educators approach these students. At the very least, it provides a cushion for failure with these kids. At its worst, it sends the message that many of the students are likely unteachable. Failure is not only likely but also can be anticipated and predicted. The very act of learning, the fundamental task of the teacher, will not occur in any more robust ways than what has happened up to that point. The current success, of course, is due to the efforts of the adults in the system. The failures, on the other hand, are both expected and not likely to find a remedy. The die has been cast. Once again, successes of others are dismissed. They are either suspiciously too good to be true or are apples and oranges to the present difficulties facing this school.

Interestingly, this attitude can even creep into the collective conscious within a school. A fourth-grade teacher cannot find success with Johnny, even though the third-grade teacher made tremendous gains with him. But that's different. For a litany of reasons, it is not the same Johnny that is now in question. Sometimes the theory pervades an entire grade. "The sophomore class is just not a group of strong writers this year." Never mind the fact that one teacher in the department has shown tremendous work product. An aberration. The computer scheduling program randomly placed all of the best kids in the same teacher's room, it would seem.

A leader must be diligent in noting and monitoring the stories that emerge in the school setting. The stories that a school tells, especially the ones that relate what cannot possibly be done, are very informative. These tender spots are the places where instructional leadership is most critical. If staff members do not bother telling a story about a problem, it may be a sign that the people are working through the difficulties and progress is being made. However, the problems with an accompanying negative story tell the tale of a system that has nearly given up trying to problem solve. Moreover, the school is putting the topic to rest by eulogizing the prospect of solving the problem by telling a story that justifies why failure was inevitable. This is where the real work begins.

It is in these moments that the leader must, once again, intervene. This faulty and destructive narrative must be dismantled and scattered to the four winds. A principal must create a very concrete and specific list of problems that are being encountered in the building setting. This list needs to be very descriptive with specific details. It should encompass the entirety of all problems and shortcomings that the system is facing. Then the principal needs to engage in an exercise with the most positive members of the building leadership team to identify one time, one occasion, or one person who has defied expectations in conquering this problem.

Who beat the odds? If the school is having an issue losing students to drop out because of teen pregnancy, the leader needs to identify *one* student who was in this circumstance who was able to get through and graduate. This becomes the bright spot and sign of hope for that problem. If Johnny is failing six of his classes, that means he is passing one. Which class is Johnny passing? What are the things that teacher is doing to find success with a young man even though most every other adult in the building continues to struggle with him?

Very rarely does a school setting experience absolutely no success with a student, a group of students, or a particular issue. Instead, it typically succeeds in some ways but fails on other occasions. This newly identified success story literally becomes the face of how these issues will be attacked in the future. It is critical to note that one person's success has proven that the school has the capacity to deal with the problem. Beyond that, the principal simply needs to figure out how to *replicate* that successful scenario with more kids and on more occasions. The principal must cite the example of success over and over. It is no longer a question of whether it can be done; it is a question of how the school can do it more reliably.

These are the kids and their stories of success that comprise the emotional scrapbooks in the hearts of all educators. When educators tell these stories, they usually begin with great pride and joy, "No one else thought this kid could do it. . . ." In this recognition resides the greatest of hope. A little bit of hope is not only a powerful thing but all that is necessary to gain a foothold into transforming the lives of kids who need it most. One small glimmer of hope changes everything.

Chapter 2

Exploring the Trenches

If a man were to come into possession of a business that supplies diamonds, it would be wise to visit the diamond mine periodically. This would be especially true if the quality of the diamonds being produced became suspect. Principals too are the caretakers of their own sort of diamonds. As it turns out, they spend a great deal of time *near* their diamond mine without necessarily getting close enough to examine it properly.

A fundamental task of any leader is to assess and examine the strengths and weaknesses of the system in a critical way. An important component of this reflection is the introspection leaders must impose upon themselves to determine their own capacity within the system. The same critical eye that the leader uses to examine teachers must also be turned inward in a very honest conversation as well. If the leader is willing to engage in this sort of self-assessment, tremendous insights can be discovered. Most often, leaders conduct a self-assessment only upon the request of their superior. Done in this manner, a leader tries to arrive at the kinds of weaknesses they may indeed possess, but only ones that the leader is willing to share with a supervisor.

Obviously, this does not always produce the most honest or thorough self-evaluation. However, if leaders are truly trying to reframe and redefine their professional environment, they must understand that they themselves are a major contributing factor. As such, the failure to recognize personal strengths and weaknesses comes at the expense of a faulty interpretation of everything and everyone who interacts with the leader because reality is viewed through a faulty lens.

Obviously, this is not easy work. No one really enjoys finding fault in themselves at any level. This is further exacerbated by the fact that educators' sense of self seems to be inextricably bound up in how they view themselves as human beings. This may not be true for every profession. There are some who work their eight-hour shift and then go about the rest of their day and define themselves by the remaining sixteen hours and not the eight hours they have just worked. This is less true for educators. Educators define themselves and their ultimate worth as people by the job they do during the day. This makes it even more difficult to establish a baseline self-assessment that is honest enough to be helpful.

The first hurdle that leaders must overcome is a humble recognition that they likely know far less about what is going on in their classrooms than they would like to admit. Principals certainly function within the school setting throughout the day and are probably in classrooms to some degree. However, being *near* a thing and truly *understanding* that thing can be very different propositions. In reality, most principals spend precious little time in the classrooms where students are learning.

Many nuances and intricacies of the classroom environment cannot be gleaned from a distance. Nor can they be appreciated and understood by doing a quick flyby in the classroom. In the interest of volume and expediency, many principals have incorporated rapid walkthroughs to establish a presence and find patterns within their school. While some presence in the classrooms is certainly better than none, the ultimate aim of classroom visits should be to learn something rather than just clock time. Perhaps there is a bit of truth in the maxim of "management by walking around." The principal might certainly notice garbage bins that need emptied and a teacher who was late to class.

However, *leadership* by walking around is not possible. Certainly, the opposite, leadership by sitting in the office, is not the answer either. Rather, as a principal begins by walking around, what happens next, or doesn't, creates the potential opportunity to lead. The most basic and honest assessment of whether a leader has committed to know the environment is easily revealed by a time audit of the calendar. While principals likely work more than an eight-hour day on a daily basis, this sort of review should be limited to the exact amount of time kids are receiving instruction in school. Likely, this amounts to anywhere from seven to eight hours in a day.

If instructional time is limited to seven hours, this equates to 420 minutes. A principal should then review a week's worth of time on the calendar and quantify the number of minutes that were spent inside a classroom. Simple math dividing the sum of these minutes by 420 will give the percentage of time spent observing kids learn. This resulting percentage should be calculated over the course of the week to get a stable and typical result. At this point, a principal should complete the following sentence: "Instructing students is the primary reason for my school's existence and I spend ____ percent of my time observing it."

This sentence is meant to evoke a visceral response. It would be a rare exception for a principal to feel very comfortable with the number of minutes calculated in the aforementioned exercise. To gain even greater perspective, it is necessary to compare the amount of minutes devoted to a presence in classrooms to other activities in which a principal might engage. For example, how does classroom observation time compare to time committed to staff meetings? Or time spent checking e-mail? Or time spent supervising kids while they eat their lunch? There is no doubt that many of the items that clutter a principal's calendar are essential. Lunch rooms must be supervised. However, many of these managerial items have multiplied to the point where they have crowded out the most essential functions happening within a school.

Most principals would agree that the work happening in classrooms is the most critical aspect of what is happening in a school, yet very little time is typically dedicated to being a part of it. The principal teacher has forgotten what the inside of the classroom feels like. This needs to be reclaimed. Principals who are serious about embracing and identifying themselves as instructional leaders must be fundamentally bothered by this imbalance in time allocation between matters that are urgent and those that are most important.

Anyone who has spent time in a modern school setting recognizes that principals are very busy professionals. The problem of principals not spending enough time in classrooms is not because they are choosing to sit idle. Indeed, most principals probably work a fifty-hour-work week and still leave unfinished work on their desk every night. A wide variety of people with varying interests try very hard to capture a principal's attention, and they are consequently pulled very thin. However, there is a way for principals to reclaim some of their time for the most important functions within their setting which may be currently neglected.

Most principals, regardless of how busy they are, are very conscientious about respecting the appointments they make with other people. For example, if a parent were to ask for a meeting with the principal for twenty minutes, the principal would certainly schedule it on his calendar and work very hard to ensure that nothing else interrupted that sacred time with the parent. Principals are also likely to set aside time for other stakeholders as well. Certainly, many of these appointments may be important to the other person but may not be the most important happenings in the school at any given time. Interestingly, conscientious principals do not choose to honor scheduled calendar commitments based upon whether they feel that the requested meeting is important. If they agree to meet during the allotted time, the promise is valued and the appointment kept.

Principals must recognize that people requesting meetings are not the only calendar items that can be established. For example, a principal is likely to set calendar events for other reasons such as dentist appointments and meetings that frequently arise. Unfortunately, most principals have not recognized that they can set appointments on other very important matters as well. The principal who is attempting to become physically present in classrooms simply must schedule a dedicated block of time in their day, every day, to ensure that this happens. One way to do this is to set a repeating calendar event every day of the work week.

The principal could choose to set aside thirty minutes every day to visit classrooms. Knowing that other commitments may interfere and not allow them to do it at the same time every day, a principal can simply slide that block of time to where it best cooperates with other commitments on the calendar. However, at this point, the principal needs to treat that appointment no different from a dentist appointment or a meeting with an angry parent. In the same way that those meetings are not lightly bumped from the calendar, classroom observation appointments should be honored as well.

Further, administrative assistants and clerical support should treat these commitments no different from other obligations. If the principal were in a meeting with a parent and a teacher asked to meet at that time, the secretary would certainly inform the teacher that they are busy at the present moment and the teacher should try to schedule a time to meet with the principal at a later time. This must also be the standard procedure when principals are engaged in classroom observations. If somebody needs to see the principal on another matter, they can certainly schedule a time, but this appointment should not be interrupted either. Thoughtful consideration should also be given to spread the times around so the principal is not viewing the same teachers at the same time every day. Failure to vary the observation schedule creates a situation that not only is limited in perspective but also does not allow for sufficient visits for teachers who have a preparatory period during the time the principal tends to do walk-throughs.

A principal will not be able to commit to an increased visible presence in classrooms if it is not supported by a strong scheduling system that carves out dedicated time every day to ensure it happens. However, principals also need to become opportunistic in seeking out ways in which they can get out of their own offices.

For example, if a principal needs to talk to students regarding attendance issues, they will often ask a secretary to send for them on a hall pass to have them come discuss the issue. Instead, a principal can gather up the pile of truancy notices and go find the students in their current location. Leaders must exercise caution, though, in not conducting a walk-through in the room where the student is. This will send a message that the principal does indeed visit classrooms, but it is for the express purpose of pulling troubled kids out of class.

Instead, principals should conduct a brief instructional walk-through next door to the class where their student is. This provides easy access for a classroom visit without equating it to being a discipline call. After the walk-through is complete, the principal can walk next door and ask that the students needing intervention step out into the hall for a walking conversation about attendance.

If the reason to run errands around the building does not include student discipline, it is much easier and straightforward in conducting observations as other tasks are completed. For example, if a principal needs to do a sweep of the parking lot as part of normal security procedures, there are a number of built-in opportunities to pop in to classrooms on the way there and back. Any time issues need attention but are not emergencies or serious discipline matters, an opportunity exists to meet others outside of closed doors. Sitting behind a desk can keep a principal constantly busy, but an analysis of many typical tasks reveals that most items can be accomplished by seeking others out rather than by summoning them to the office. A principal will soon find that this approach of weaving classroom observations into the normal course of business does not feel like an extra burden. In actuality, it becomes reinvigorating as many positive and uplifting chances to see kids at their best become intermixed with inevitable occasions to work kids through discipline matters.

Principals can easily find themselves caught in the pinch between needing to know what is going on in their buildings and the very real fact that they are not spending enough time in each classroom to form a proper opinion. This can create a very dangerous set of circumstances. Because principals need to have an opinion of their teachers, they end up forming one even if they lack firsthand observations. When people are in social situations where the interaction and knowledge of those around them do not matter a great deal, they can afford to put very little thought into their opinion of that person. The principal simply does not have that luxury.

Every teacher is ultimately under their direction and they need to have a way to characterize each individual. Unfortunately, leaders often allow secondhand and thirdhand information to creep into their belief system about others when they lack their own firsthand knowledge. Not only is this unfair to the teacher, but it also can create unhealthy work place settings if the principal is treating others a certain way based on what they believe to be true. Further, it is even more dangerous if a principal begins to make decisions in light of what they believe to be true. The following example is illustrative of the kinds of events that play out in public school classrooms each day when a guidance counselor walks into Mr. Williams' office and asks for a minute of his time.

Counselor: "You need to do something about Mr. Jones."

Principal: "What do you mean?"

Counselor: "He is so mean to kids. I don't know how we allow an adult to treat kids that way in our school in this day and age."

Principal: "What is he doing?"

Counselor: "Oh, he is very aloof and does not connect well with kids at all."

Principal: "What does he do specifically?"

Counselor: "Well, when he sees them make a mistake, he'll snap at them and say I told you not to do it that way or he will roll his eyes at them if they ask a question he thinks is dumb."

Principal: "That goes against all of our training on teacher–student relationships."

Counselor: "I know. Kids cannot stand him. They all want to leave his class. He is not even on continuing contract. You're the boss but I don't think you should renew his contract. We could do better."

Obviously, the counselor in this scenario has very strong opinions that the principal may or may not share. Even if the principal does not ultimately pursue the termination of the teacher, the seed has been planted in his own mind that Mr. Jones is struggling. How would this conversation have been different if the principal would have asked additional questions:

How many kids have complained?
Could the counselor provide a specific example?
Has the counselor talked to any other kids who are in the class who have not come in yet?
Has the counselor ever dropped by the classroom to see any of this firsthand?

Clearly, principals receive reports like this daily and would only be making a mistake if they conclude that the report is the end of the story and not the beginning. The principal is compelled in moments like this to gather firsthand information. How does this report match up with what has been witnessed firsthand already?

Reports like the one the principal received might be true. More likely, however, they only contain a measure of truth and the complexity of what is really happening is missing. The description of someone's behavior, however inappropriate it may be, is fully understood only when viewing it within the context in which it happened. Reports like this can never portray the context for what it truly is. This does not excuse bad behavior on the part of adults. On the contrary, the full context of the situation may end up painting an even worse picture of what is happening. The point is that secondhand accounts, no matter how well intentioned they may be, are always inaccurate simply because they are incomplete. By definition, they are always incomplete.

Fortunately, principals do not have to rely upon secondhand accounts to form the basis of their opinions. Aside from events that happened only once, principals always have the ability to begin observing for themselves what is happening in classrooms. For the purposes of improving the instructional experience in the classroom, the principal theoretically is able to begin accruing accurate information all day and every day.

Because school personnel tend to speak so freely about their peers, principals need to take great caution in reaching conclusions about their employees. In fact, one healthy activity principals can engage in is to mentally list the characteristics and attributes of their teachers. After each characteristic, they should try to determine how it is they believe the teacher possesses that quality. Further, the principal should reflect on whether that quality was observed firsthand or relayed by others. Even if it were firsthand information from personal observations, a principal should ask how often that quality has been observed. One has to wonder why certain events were so memorable in the first place. Sometimes, it is because it is such a unique quality. Other times, it is because it was a behavior that validated an opinion the principal thought to be true.

After a principal lists the characteristics of the teacher and determines how it is they came to know that about the teacher, the next step is to determine if those qualities are always present or only under certain circumstances. This makes a big difference. Everybody can find themself in the sort of stressful situations where they behave in a way that is not typical and is not representative of the way they normally act. It is a shame when a principal's opinion of a teacher is based upon one event that was triggered by a rare and stressful occasion.

Teachers deserve better than this. If they are struggling in any way within the classroom, they deserve to have an instructional leader who understands them for what is actually true and who they truly are. It is promising to note that any mistakes a principal has made in the past in rushing to judgment about a teacher based upon incomplete or secondhand information is easily remedied. However, it does not happen by accident. The principal must take deliberate and concerted efforts to validate their own opinions in a way that is rooted in facts. Not only is this approach the most reasonable way to proceed with an employee, but also it is the only way to improve the system in a genuine way. Principals are tasked with very personal work when leading instruction. To do so in a way that is not rooted in honesty and firsthand experience will be immediately dismissed by those who need help the most.

As important as it is to know and understand teachers as accurately as possible, it is also critical that principals understand how to begin to appear more frequently in their environment in a healthy way. Much like the saying within the medical profession, a principal should "first do no harm." If the principal is truly desiring to transform their own practices and begin increasing their visibility within the classrooms of the school and this has not been their current practice, it will certainly be met with some angst and confusion in the beginning. If a teacher has the lived experience of seeing their principal once every few weeks and begins seeing him on a daily basis, it would not be a surprise if the anxiety within the faculty increases dramatically.

Of course, this can be remedied if principals front-load their work by having honest conversations with the faculty in advance of adopting new behaviors themselves. The principal must speak in honest yet convincing ways letting them know that the underlying purpose for the increased presence in the classroom is rooted in a sincere desire to better understand the challenges and struggles of teachers. Not only can a principal send a message that will show appreciation for what is happening within the school, but it can also send a strong message that the principal intends to help teachers in new ways.

Of course, in order to help, a principal first needs to understand. It is important for a principal to communicate this message to the entire faculty as a group so that no individual feels as if they are being targeted. In this moment, a principal cannot afford to have the staff begin to divide believing that some are favored while others are receiving deeper scrutiny than ever. Instead, the principal should send a very clear message that they simply want to understand everything and everyone better. This does not mean, of course, that everyone will believe the rationale, but it will certainly create the necessary foundation to begin engaging in a different behavior because it has been explained beforehand. The principal should take great care in the beginning to make note of troubling incidents or patterns that are observed but should respond to them in very deliberate ways. Otherwise, the teachers' worst fears will be confirmed that the increased presence was a ploy to hammer teachers in a negative way.

Once a principal has laid the groundwork in communicating the new behaviors that can be expected, the next step is to follow through by increasing visibility within the classes. However, in these beginning stages, it is important to recognize that the response from both teachers and the students will not be authentic. For their part, teachers are likely to respond in a number of negative ways when a leader increases their presence in the classroom. Some teachers will get nervous and begin talking and acting in ways that are not typical of their normal behavior. It is important for principals to recognize that very little information that is useful can be gathered if the teacher is not acting naturally in these moments. Principals need to be prepared to dismiss much of what they observe of teachers in these early stages.

The only true usefulness in the short term may be in acclimating the teacher to the principal's presence within the room.

Other teachers may respond in irritation or anger to their environment becoming disrupted. Principals should guard against the inclination to build rapport by interacting with teachers who are showing signs of irritation. While it may put the nervous teacher at ease, the irritated teacher may use the interaction as evidence of the disruptive nature of the principal's presence in the room. This, of course, is counterproductive. Rather, principals should pay very close attention to the dynamics of the classroom and make sure that their presence is not a disruption to the teacher. This is accomplished by the ways in which principals position themselves within the room and their body language while they are observing.

Every bit of body language can unintentionally send a message to a teacher who is likely trying to glean bits of feedback from their leader. One way a principal can know if the increased visibility has hit a point of sufficient familiarity is when teachers no longer ask if the principal needs something during the short visit to the classroom. In the beginning, teachers will invariably ask if there is anything that the principal needs. In time, however, teachers will not associate the presence of the principal with a related break in the action.

Likewise, the principal needs to be very careful in their interaction with students in these moments. If a principal has not had much of a presence within the classroom setting, most students are going to automatically conclude that the principal is in the room because somebody is in trouble. Of course, students are not shy in blurting out their theories on who the guilty party is and this can be a tremendous disruption to the flow of instruction. Even if students do not assume that somebody is in trouble, the presence of another adult, especially the principal of the school, can amp up the anxiety within the students as well. This can manifest by students acting and behaving in ways contrary to the natural classroom environment. This is not to say that they will necessarily misbehave, but they may simply act in ways contrary to normal classroom functioning.

Once again, a principal needs to recognize that very little accurate information may be gathered in this moment and instead the classroom visit is simply an investment in developing familiarity. Principals will know when their presence comes with a sufficient amount of ease when students not only stay on task when the principal enters but also persist in their engagement even when the principal moves in closer to examine their actual work. Likewise, a new level is achieved when students freely offer comments and discussion without telling glances toward their principal to check for a reaction.

At this point, a principal may begin to observe genuine student and teacher activities in the classroom, but great caution must still be exercised as many variables still need to be considered. While teachers must be observed in a genuine way in an authentic environment, principals must recognize that even teachers who are consistent in their approach and delivery within the classroom exhibit a wide variety of styles and behaviors. First, the principal needs to take into account the variety of courses a teacher may be assigned. If a principal is observing an elementary teacher, the leader must consider that the way in which the teacher functions in a language arts lesson may be quite different from a mathematics lesson.

Likewise, if the principal is observing a secondary teacher, they may be assigned a wide variety of courses within a specific discipline. For example, a person may describe themself as a high school social studies teacher. In reality though, the actual courses that the person teaches are quite diverse. This teacher could teach U.S. government, world history, psychology, and current events. Without question, teaching psychology is a very different proposition than teaching world history. It is quite likely that the same person will be assigned that breath of coursework within their discipline.

A principal should take opportunities to ensure that the observations of teachers are not limited to one specific course of study. It is quite likely that different nuances will emerge depending upon the course being taught. This helps to add a breadth and depth to a principal's understanding of the strengths and weaknesses of a given teacher. Similarly, a principal must take into account both the age and developmental level of the students that the teacher is teaching. Although an elementary teacher may not have more than a year between the youngest and oldest student in the classroom, teaching assignments may change from year to year and a teacher may be responsible for many different developmental levels of students depending upon the given year. Secondary teachers, of course, could easily have a span of student ages as much as four to five years throughout the day or even within a given classroom period. Aside from the fact that this creates quite a challenge for teachers, a principal should take careful notes on any patterns that emerge when observing a teacher of different groups of kids.

It would seem that some teachers have a sweet spot where they function best with an age group of kids. Some teachers seem to be wired to teach very advanced students, while others seem to thrive with kids who struggle on a daily basis. Obviously, teachers rarely have the luxury of teaching a singular type, age, or ability level of student. The work of a teacher is with an incredibly wide group and often does not account for that teacher's favored group. This can create difficulties if the teacher tends to gravitate toward the type of student with whom they have the greatest interest and ability.

In these situations, a principal can conduct a classroom observation and note a wide variety of experiences within the same time and space depending upon the student. Large variation in the lived experience among students in a classroom can be very troubling. The teacher who is viewed as highly effective with one student may not be producing good results with another. While some dominant patterns tend to arise, a principal is usually quite surprised when they hear that a teacher is the favorite of a particular student when others complain about the teacher frequently. Noting the patterns for a given teacher within a classroom setting is important in taking into account the complexity of what is happening in the room at any given time.

Then complexity of what a principal may experience even extends to the time of day and season of the year as well. Some teachers start out strong and lose steam as the year progresses. Others take a while to develop ease within the class, building rapport at a slower rate. On a smaller scale, some teachers seem to function as a different person in the morning than they do in the afternoon. While people often joke about the fact that they are not a morning person, what if that is the only time in which a student interacts with that teacher? If a principal doesn't observe the teacher at different times during the instructional day, much of this nuance is missed.

Principals can often experience a blind spot in their observations of teachers depending upon their teaching style. Most principals spent a certain amount of time in the classroom as teachers themselves before transitioning into an administrative position. With that experience comes a development of their own voice as a teacher within the classroom. As principals experience success in their own classrooms as teachers earlier in their career, they can develop a biased opinion of quality instruction in the classroom. If the principal happened to maintain a classroom that was very orderly and did not encourage much conversation among students, an art classroom where students are scurrying about the room gathering supplies and collaborating with peers could be viewed as complete chaos. Some classrooms can indeed be chaotic, but busy classrooms are not necessarily so.

Each type of classroom style may be labeled differently depending upon the preferences of the principal. A loud classroom may be described as vibrant by some, out of control by others. A quiet classroom could be considered restrictive by some, focused by others. Teacher characteristics should not be pigeonholed and over-generalized, and the same is true for classroom dynamics.

Classrooms that lack coherent instruction are never beneficial, but deciding that a given approach lacks coherency demands thoughtful consideration. The cardinal mistake that principals make in this regard is to have a bias toward their own preferred instructional approach. Teachers who remind the principal of themself are not necessarily better teachers. Even if a principal is mature and thoughtful enough to recognize this, it is also important that the principal develop a comfort level within a classroom environment where he or she is not necessarily comfortable at first. In these classrooms, the leader may not instinctively recognize the aspects of the classroom that are working. In a room that is reminiscent of their former classrooms, anything familiar will register as good practice.

In classrooms with a more foreign approach to the leader, the principal needs to engage in self-talk to recognize good things. For example, a principal may say, "I never let students do that in my classroom. Is it producing a favorable experience for students? What are the students doing that would indicate that it is a good experience? How might this approach be producing a better result than the way I'd do it? How much is my personal comfort level influencing my perspective on what is happening here?"

Assuming that the principal is committed to an increased presence of the classroom, has taken pains to schedule regular and frequent opportunities to do so, and has gotten past the awkwardness of engaging in these new behaviors with all students and staff, the leader can now begin in earnest to feel like genuine observations can be made. Once again, principals must take great care in how they proceed in this new environment. There are many ways to proceed at this point. Where exactly should a principal fixate their attention?

The first distinction to make is whether the principal is observing the teacher or the students. When a principal is observing a teacher, there are a number of things to notice and observe. First, principals should note the manner in which teachers carry themselves in the classroom. Are they meek or are they assertive? Do they engage in light banter with kids or do they immediately get down to business? These affective behaviors are important to note. In these moments, principals must recognize that they should suspend all judgment. Instead, they should take great pains to refrain from drawing any conclusions upon what they see. Rather, they should simply collect observations. Where does the teacher stand? Does the teacher ever sit down? What kind of questions does the teacher ask the students?

There is both a depth and breadth of what teachers are trying to accomplish in the classroom, and a principal must try to decide what they are seeing and what it is telling them about the classroom experience for kids. Likewise, principals should record observations of what they see the students doing as well. Are the students excited or reluctant to be in the room? Do they engage with the teacher or pull back and withdraw within themselves during the class time? Principals should note whether students are actively interested in answering the questions that a teacher poses or whether they have to be forced to engage. Do the same students answer all of the questions? Do students raise their hands to engage even if they are confused and do not know the answer?

One powerful observation principals can use to assess student engagement without making judgments is by assessing student engagement at regular intervals for a given period of time. For example, a principal can choose the frequency of observation. Typically, it is every thirty seconds if they are only there for short period of time or it could be once every two minutes if they intend to stay in the classroom for longer period. Regardless of the interval, a principal waits for the time chosen to lapse and simply does a quick calculation of how many students are in the room and how many are actively engaged in learning when the clock expires.

This is repeated at the chosen interval, and the pattern is noted at the end of the engagement exercise. By choosing a predetermined time interval, a principal has an unbiased way of noting the way in which engagement waxes and wanes throughout the lesson. Again, this should be done without judgment yet. Instead, the principal is able to leave with the interesting observation that, on average, 46 percent of the students were engaged during the lesson.

Because the principal has made prior investment in being present in the classroom a sufficient number of times that students' anxiety levels have not been increased, a principal should freely engage with students when appropriate during these observations. An easy but informative icebreaker for principals is to simply ask a student what they are learning in that moment. Principals should note if students are able to answer this question. Perhaps students mechanically refer to an objective that has placed upon the board as their answer. Others may engage in a genuine dialogue about what they're learning and how that fits in with other things in the class. It should be noted that throughout all of these observations, the principal should not yet be attaching an opinion or conclusion on how the lesson is going. Whether the instruction is good enough or if sufficient learning is happening is a different exercise than honing observational skills.

A willingness to simply identify what is being observed before trying to understand or explain it is the fairest way to ensure that the principal is not rushing to judgment on what is happening in the classroom. When the principal tries to piece together what is being observed, it is important to note that every insight should be accompanied by direct observations to support the opinion. For example, if a principal is trying to discern whether the students responded better to direct instruction than a subsequent discussion, mental evidence should be offered to justify that assertion.

It appeared that half of the classroom was doodling on their notebook paper during the lecture, but every student except two participated by offering comments during the following discussion. This sort of direct evidence can preclude any personal preferences or biases in how the principal might have thought the lesson should have been approached, and instead, focuses the observation on the best evidence of student engagement and achievement that can be observed at that time.

Many of these exercises may seem to overly complicate the very simple act of visiting classrooms. There could be nothing further from the truth. To start, principals do not need to have a physical presence just so they can claim they are there. If this is the only motivation, it would be better to forgo the inevitable, but hopefully slight, distraction of going into the classroom. These visits should be for a great purpose and that purpose is predicated on collecting unbiased and useful information as objectively as possible. Likewise, these techniques do not require extensive or complicated record keeping. With a bit of practice, most of the observations at this point could be organized mentally. In fact, collecting extensive notes during these moments could actually increase anxiety in both teachers and students. If a teacher has finally accepted the fact that a principal is now in the classroom, imagine how that teacher's mind could race wondering what is being written about their performance.

When leaders try to establish coherence in their own understanding of a situation, they often do so by trying to find patterns to confirm what they believe is happening. Observing the same teachers on multiple occasions at various times of day in different content areas is a great start to making that happen. These observations are often confirmed by subsequent conversations with the teacher about what happened during the observation. However, there is often even more to the story than what has been gathered up to this point. Imagine the following interaction between the principal and the teacher after a brief classroom visit.

Teacher: "Hey, thanks for stopping in to my classroom today."

Principal: "I thoroughly enjoyed it."

Teacher: "I thought it went pretty well except I'm sure you noticed that Victor was pretty disengaged throughout the lesson."

Principal: "Yeah, I did happen to notice. What's going on with him?"

Teacher: "Well, you know his home life is a mess, and he seems really distracted. I'm trying to be firm but gentle with him right now. I'm afraid he's using it as an excuse to be a bit lazy though."

What should a principal make of this theory that the teacher is proposing? Certainly, the principal did indeed witness Victor disengage throughout the lesson. It is now up to the principal to investigate a bit further to determine how accurate the portrayal of this classroom dynamic actually is. The next step for the principal to take is to look at Victor's current grades. Is he failing all classes as poorly as this one? Chances are that, however poor his grades may be, they are not all exactly the same. Oftentimes, there will be a wide variance from class to class in overall performance. This principal's next stop should be to the classroom where Victor is performing the best.

Before speaking to the teacher, the principal should witness firsthand how Victor conducts himself in this class. Sometimes the exact same behaviors will be witnessed, but if he is doing better in this class, it is often the case that the first teacher's story simply does not explain the entire truth of Victor's reality. While Victor may indeed have some difficulties at home, it is a rush to judgment to suppose that the behavior that Victor is exhibiting in one classroom is a standard way of behaving at all times in all places. This creates an incredible opportunity for further conversation with the original teacher. Being diplomatic and tactful is essential, but relating the information that Victor is quite engaged in other classrooms is a great opportunity to rewrite the narrative about what must be going on with the student and why.

The sweeping narratives explaining student behavior are not necessarily limited to specific individual students. Oftentimes, narratives explaining behavior or performance can extend to entire classes or grade levels. Teachers will often say things like, "You know these seventh graders this year are just very poor writers." Another common example is, "This fifth-grade class has been a behavioral problem from the very beginning. Go ask the first-grade teachers how they always act."

Principals must guard against these group generalizations just as they must question individual student judgments. Once again, principals are compelled to investigate these theories at a deeper level by finding those moments and occasions where the theory does not hold true. Which students in the aforementioned examples could be found who are above average writers? How many students in that fifth-grade class are not behavior problems at all? The principal must then observe carefully to figure out why the supposed pattern does not hold true under these other encouraging situations. Identifying patterns can be very useful, but knowing the circumstances under which the pattern does not hold true is not only essential but also the key to replicating the desired outcome.

The final aspect to be explored as a principal establishes the lay of the land is the dynamics between groups of teachers. Every physical location where people repeatedly gather develops its own culture. This culture can be influenced and shaped by the actions of a strong leader. It can also develop when a school leader allows other voices to emerge in the space, creating a vastly different culture than the one the leader desires.

Before efforts can be made to redefine the culture among groups of teachers, the principal needs to understand the prevailing climate in the school. Much like the way the principal carefully observes students in the school setting, principals need to observe the way teachers act and interact in the environment. There are many places and occasions where people may choose to gather at work. Historically, the teachers' lounge has been a place set aside for adults to gather when they are not busy working with kids. Schools are often known for the horror stories about questionable and destructive conversations that occur in this space.

Groups gather at other times and spaces throughout the school as well. Teachers with common preparatory periods may congregate and discuss their professional lives. Teachers who share the same common office spaces may do the same. Many times, teachers develop their own relationships and alliances that transcend proximity. Principals would do well to notice and understand the way these groups come together and how they function as a collective unit. Principals may find that unlikely personalities find each other as they establish common ground around the things they find important. On occasion, strong and positive group dynamics form around dedicated educators who wish to collaborate with their peers. At other times, negativity and pessimism can be the uniting force among teacher groups.

Principals must take steps to understand what topics tend to bring groups together and the dynamics that emerge within that group. For example, one group of teachers is frustrated with the principal's response to minor rule violations. Another group of teachers comes together to ruminate on better instructional practices and how to reach difficult students. These two groups inform the leader of entirely different things about the mind-set of teachers and what they see as the most important problems to address. Regardless of the truth surrounding these conversations, an understanding of what topics dominate the discussion is essential. An understanding of this group dynamic helps a principal understand the current thinking of groups of teachers, which is equally as important as the mind-set of individual teachers operating within their own classroom. A leader who desires to move the system must pay attention to and consider both.

Principals should not overreact to their initial assessment of the behaviors and mentality driving the culture and climate of their building. Indeed, both positive and negative attitudes and opinions can evolve over time depending on a number of factors. Some of these reasons are superficial and transient and will likely come and go as days go by. A leader must be able to recognize the difference between temporary frustration and deeply held attitudes which are in conflict with the mission and vision of the school. Allowing people to vent their temporary frustrations is a healthy thing. Leaders should not make too much of these moments and assume that they aren't representative of anything more than a bad day. Whenever large numbers of people intersect in an emotionally charged environment, frustrations are bound to emerge.

The principal must take great care that new decisions do not get made in response to a fleeting concern. Principals may need to steel themselves against these constant gripes that are brought forward. It can certainly take the energy and positivity out of life if days are spent capturing one negative comment after another. A leader must recognize moments when people just need to vent, and redirect them in the moments where they start to perseverate on the wrong kinds of things. More than anything, leaders cannot get frustrated or discourage themselves from being surrounded by negativity. Leaders must use extreme caution that they do not begin adapting their own behavior in an effort to steer around these negative people. When principals are in the midst of developing sound, positive habits regarding teacher observations, the worst mistake that can happen is that the principal begins to prefer certain classrooms over others.

There is no doubt that some classrooms will refresh and reinvigorate the leader's spirit and these classrooms are often the model for the entire building. Principals do indeed need to spend a fair amount of time in these rooms, but they need to spend as much or more time in the rooms that need more of their assistance. Wellness checks are important, but they cannot eclipse the need for the academic physician to bring assistance to those who most need it. Not only does this bias toward some bring about ill-will within the faculty where some are seen as favorites, but it also begins to isolate everyone in academic silos dividing the haves and the have-nots.

The only way to ensure that a leader is not falling into bad habits in this regard is to build a schedule that keeps the process honest. If the principal has recognized that more time is needed to be spent in classrooms, a commitment was made to build daily observations in to the calendar. At this step, principals need to track these observations to determine not only where they have been, but where they need to go next.

Every principal has preferences of where they would like to spend their observation time, but until it is seen on paper, the patterns showing which teachers and content areas are being neglected sometimes is not as readily visible. Accurate records of classroom visits are essential in this process. Leaders should conduct a weekly review to determine if all grade levels are receiving equal treatment. After that is determined, principals should check to see if all subject areas have been observed. Beyond that, principals should ensure that all teachers have been seen and that, in the next round, the principal should commit to see them at a different time of day.

If principals commit to the type of thorough review of the educational landscape that has been entrusted to their care, it provides critical foundations for more impactful work. An honest admission of the current lack of time and focus spent in classrooms, coupled with a firm commitment to build authentic opportunities into daily operations, is an incredibly sound beginning. When this work is followed up by unbiased observations that are rooted in a genuine desire to understand, principals can begin to build instructional credibility.

Judgments about what is happening and what should be done next are for another day. These preliminary steps are about building true and accurate knowledge of what is really happening in the building.

Inevitably, this work leads to very difficult conversations with teachers. There is no getting away from the fact that this work will quickly reveal poor behaviors and practices. Additionally, the work may reveal negative and destructive philosophical beliefs that teachers have about children and their role as educators. As painful and difficult as these crossroads will be, they will at least be confronted and exposed in honesty and truth.

A tired and well-worn excuse for teachers who are underperforming with kids is that the principal "doesn't know what is going on" or that the principal "doesn't understand."

Unfortunately, in the past, this was often true. Principals did not always have firsthand evidence of what was happening in their own schools. A teacher could be engaged in terrible instructional practices and when questioned by the principal, the teacher could create a weak defense by saying, "How would the principal know what's really going on, he has only been in my classroom twice this year?"

This teacher is correct that the principal does not truly know what is going on. However, that is not to say that the teacher is justified in the behavior. All that can be concluded from this exchange is that the principal currently lacks the firsthand understanding that brings enough credibility to solve the problem for what it truly is. These sort of objections will forever be put to rest after proper foundations are laid. Moving forward, principals will still be confronted with extremely difficult and complex conversations and work. However, the leader will now be able to get to the true heart of the matter to help kids.

Chapter 3

Gathering Available Resources

In order to move the instructional conversation forward at this point in the new conception of the principal's work, a leader needs to begin to assess what all of these observations are revealing about the instructional practices in the school. In order to do this, principals must begin to compare what they are witnessing in the classroom against best practices. In the same way that the principal began this work with a humble realization of the lack of intimate knowledge of the inner-workings of classrooms due to limited occasions in observing teachers, principals must also deeply reflect on their own strengths and weaknesses in instructional knowledge and abilities. Principals are on the threshold of powerful conversations regarding what they witness in the classroom. In order to be prepared to engage in these deep and often difficult conversations, principals must take a thorough inventory of the tools they themselves are bringing into the conversation.

The first key insight for principals to understand about themselves and all others in their profession is that people know *how* to teach better than they typically *do* on any given day. This observation deserves some deep reflection to process how fundamentally true it is for all aspects of life. People know how to eat healthier than they usually do. People typically know how to be a better parent or spouse than they tend to be on any given day. This is not as scathing of an indictment against others as it may appear to be. It is no surprise that everyone possesses a far greater capacity for excellence than they are able to sustain day in and day out.

Before a principal turns this insight onto their consideration of others, they first must look inward and seek the truth of this observation in their own professional life. In what ways does a principal know how to do the job more effectively than they may be operating on any given day? This exercise is worth listing out in great detail. Likely, there are some professional areas where a principal excels and does so on a daily basis. This is likely a badge of honor that a principal takes great pride in, and rightfully so.

For example, a principal may take great pride in their commitment to communicating well with parents. They may maintain a blog, send out frequent newsletters, and pride themself on returning parent phone calls immediately. She greets parents warmly at school activities and builds a strong rapport with all of them. As powerful as this aspect of the job may be, there are obviously many other responsibilities where the principal exerts less focus. Paying attention to both areas of excellence and areas of struggle helps portray the most accurate picture of the principal's skill set.

Throughout this exercise, a principal must reflect on whether areas of weakness are because the leader knows how to perform at high levels but does not typically do so, or whether it is a genuine gap in their own expertise. Areas where a principal can excel if they choose to simply require a commitment to focus and extend additional energies to perform at higher levels. Conversely, areas where a principal is currently lacking require a different sort of approach to bridge needed skills.

Hopefully, principals realize that their own gap between how they can perform at their very best and how they tend to perform on a normal day is not necessarily a sign of laziness or lack of commitment. Mustering focus to perform at optimal levels in all aspects of a job takes incredible focus and discipline. Leaders must examine which skills are the most critical and are likely to leverage the most powerful results to make the most intelligent decisions. Everybody has a limited amount of energy and mental bandwidth. It would be a monumental mistake to summon the focus on less than critical aspects of the job while allowing essential elements to fade into the background. This can easily happen without maintaining a diligent effort to focus on the most important and consequential elements of education.

Often, less important educational topics bring less controversy and difficulty with them. It is easy to bring major focus to minor topics. The most important work must be identified and principals must fix their attention on it. In education, people who are noisy often command the most attention. Leaders must analyze everything that could command their attention and focus efforts wisely.

Principals must recognize that this tendency to underperform is not just true for themselves but is also true for other well-meaning, dedicated educators. If principals begin this work properly by observing teachers objectively without making prior judgments about what they see, they must eventually transition to a point where they start making sense of what they have observed. In doing so, they must determine if areas of weakness they begin to observe are true gaps in the teacher's skill set. When leaders observe teachers, they must take note of areas of perceived weakness in a teacher's abilities and match them against subsequent observations and other data they are able to gather. As the principal becomes better acquainted with the strengths and weaknesses of the teachers in the building, there is an accompanying obligation to help others get better.

Developing a sound understanding of whether teachers need assistance because they are lacking a skill or if they are actually capable of performing at higher levels is sometimes difficult to discern. However, this becomes a critical juncture for the well-meaning principal. Much like a physician, the leader must be very deliberate in diagnosing potential problems in an effort to prescribe the proper remedy. When patients are reluctant to disclose their symptoms or provide incomplete descriptions of their underlying struggles, it becomes difficult to provide an appropriate response. Much like diagnosing medical conditions, getting to the bottom of the limits of a teacher's true ability level is difficult work. It is a rare person who is willing to reveal the limits of their own ability and understanding to themselves, let alone their supervisor. When a principal leads others by first discussing and revealing their own areas of struggle, it makes for a more honest conversation where the truth can emerge.

Aside from conversations that principals initiate, leaders are often asked to weigh in on critical instructional matters because of their formal leadership position. Indeed, the very direction a school takes can depend upon the position a leader chooses to take on an issue. For example, consider this conversation between a principal and a high school reading teacher:

Teacher: "Thanks for seeing me. I know you are busy, but this is very important."

Principal: "Absolutely. What is your concern?"

Teacher: "I'm sure you are aware of what we mean by the reading wars?"

Principal: "Actually, I'm not sure I do. Can you explain?"

Teacher: "Well, historically, there have been very strong opinions on how to teach students to read most effectively. There are two main camps: a whole language approach and phonics-based instruction. Some people are in one or the other of the camps or someplace in-between. Regardless of where a teacher falls on the spectrum, they usually have very strong opinions."

Principal: "I'm sorry. I was a high school social studies teacher before I became a principal. I'm afraid I don't have a whole lot of background on this subject."

Teacher: "Well, we have a problem. You know there are three of us who teach reading and we all are in very different places. Mrs. Williams believes in whole language, Ms. Thomas is a hard-core phonics believer, and I take a more balanced approach somewhere in the middle."

Principal: "So what do you see as the problem?"

Teacher: "The other two are refusing to collaborate with each other because their approaches are so different that they cannot find any common ground. Both of them will barely speak to me and that is only because they are trying to recruit me to their side. Mrs. Williams told me that to do it any other way shows a lack of integrity and that we must not really care about kids. Ms. Thomas basically said the same thing."

Principal: "How can I help?"

Teacher: "We are getting ready to adopt a reading curriculum, and I do not believe that we are capable of arriving at a sound decision."

Principal: "Can't everyone do it their own way? Live and let live."

Teacher: "The curriculum we are buying this spring will support one of the philosophies. I think you need to weigh in on this as our instructional leader. The future of our most struggling kids depends on how you resolve which approach we should be taking. I want to know what you think is best."

The leader in this dialogue is facing a very difficult instructional decision. While the principal can certainly bring other voices into the conversation for their opinion and advice, a decision must ultimately be made. Many leaders may recognize that, like the principal in the scenario, they too are ill-equipped to make a decision. However, not making a decision is, in fact, a decision. So too is deferring the decision to another time. Also, leaving a philosophically divided group with irreconcilable differences to arrive at a decision without assistance makes a strong leadership statement as well. This leader may decide to put additional efforts into working with the group to help them get along better. Indeed, that is probably quite necessary. But that approach also largely skirts the real issue. That is, students deserve the strongest reading curriculum that has the greatest possibility to assist students to function in society in a literate manner. Like the teacher in the scenario, it is a fair question to ask what the leader believes is the best option.

Most leaders would flinch when they are put to the question in this way. Some would rationalize that it is not their decision to make because they are not the expert. Indeed, at that very moment, they likely are not the expert. However, it still begs the question of whether the principal has a moral and ethical obligation to become more of an expert on areas outside of their current area of expertise. After all, this principal was a social studies teacher by training.

Perhaps, the principal was an exemplary social studies teacher. At the point where their assignment was social studies, it was enough to be a highly competent teacher in that discipline. However, upon choosing to accept the principalship, the principal immediately requires a new professional set of obligations to become more involved in content in areas where they may have very little professional experience. There is no doubt that this can seem quite daunting. The only other alternative for a leader is to outsource the most important decisions throughout their building on every possible topic outside the focus of their undergraduate degree.

This approach relegates the principal back into the role of building manager. This, of course, is the very role that the principal is trying very hard to move beyond. A leader should not systematically outsource all of the most important decisions for the future of their building to others. True leaders would certainly take the time to gather other opinions on the matter but would ultimately own these decisions themselves.

While this task may seem at first a bit overwhelming, there are a number of steps that principals can take to build their professional capacity to aid in their ability to become leaders on all important decisions. Once again, principals must have the courage to self-assess what their professional gaps and weaknesses may be in a very honest manner. This is not a time to feel discouraged about a lack of skill, but an opportunity to highlight any professional gaps and address areas in need of additional focus and training. Principals often tell both teachers and students of the importance of embracing a mind-set of being a lifelong learner. This is a moment where principals must accept the fact that they need to review what they know and what they think they know about the work of other professionals in their building. Before they get into the particulars of individual content areas, principals must review the true fundamentals of teaching and learning before considering content-specific questions.

Regardless of the content area, there are a number of elements to classroom practices that are matters of primary concern. For example, the quality of curriculum, questioning technique, instructional strategies, and assessment practices will always be of paramount importance. Principals must review their own understanding of these areas to determine if they need to learn or relearn these essentials. It is important to remain well grounded in these fundamentals.

Keeping the most important aspects of instruction in the forefront of the mind is critical because it is very easy to make mistakes about what is being witnessed when visiting a classroom outside an area of expertise. For example, suppose a principal were to visit a middle school science classroom and witnessed the students gathered around their work stations building model rockets. If the principal noted that all twenty-five students were actively engaged in the construction of them, it may be easy to conclude that all is well in the world of science.

However, a deeper reflection is in order. The first question a principal should ask is which science class was meeting. How the principal may feel about things should be entirely different if it were a life science rather than an earth science class. Certainly, earth science might make sense in a way that life science simply would not. The principal must dig even deeper, however. Knowing the learning objective as it relates to the state standards in science would provide even better information. At this point, the principal needs to guard against "the danger of -ish." The danger of -ish is the way a principal can be fooled into believing powerful learning is occurring in a class when it feels like something that would be appropriate to see is indeed observed in a given class. Building rockets feels science-ish. Watching a documentary feels history-ish. Principals must look past the superficial resemblance an activity has to the discipline being taught in order to examine whether the right things are being taught or if the teacher is merely staying within a recognizable ballpark.

For this reason, principals must ensure that teachers are well acquainted in the language of their state standards. This practice has been both embraced and despised by the educational community. In its least controversial form, the standards of a discipline are simply the promises educators make to parents and students about what students will learn. Educators promise that the focus of the year's instruction in a given class will be the thoughtful execution of established state standards. These are, after all, the body of learning that educators are required by statute to teach. Not only does a thorough understanding of state standards orient a teacher in a way that focuses coherent instruction, but it is also a common language on which principals and teachers can utilize to understand the daily happenings in the classroom.

Obviously, principals will never commit to memory the standards for a wide variety of disciplines. Rather, they need to be living documents that can refresh the principal's understanding of where teachers are likely spending their instructional time at any given moment. They become living documents when they are incorporated into district curriculum documents and daily lesson plans. For this reason, principals must insist that teachers reference their daily learning objectives back to a state standard. This creates a strong and appropriate beginning when developing lessons and gives both the students and an observing principal their bearings for what is likely to happen in the class. It would be a mistake to assume that the only purpose for standards-referenced learning targets is to help establish the topic for the day's lesson. Principals must recognize that there is a stronger and deeper opportunity to ascertain the quality of instruction buried within the language of the standards themselves. Depending upon the choice of verbs that standards documents employ to describe proficiency, all educators are able to determine the cognitive depth where they must align their instruction.

For example, if the standard requires students to *describe* a phenomenon, a specific depth of thinking is required. This is in stark contrast to a standard that may ask students to *predict* a phenomenon. There is a distinct difference in cognitive demand between describing and predicting an event. Depending upon the expectation of the standard, principals should expect a very different instructional approach within the classroom. Attending to this level of understanding is every bit as important as a teacher staying true to a standards-focused topic for the day.

Returning back to the model rocket building lab, the principal's observation of this highly engaged classroom of students demands a much deeper analysis. Seeing a class that feels science-ish is a very good start. This must be followed up by a review of the day's learning target. This, in turn, must be linked to an appropriate state science standard. Supposing all of those elements seem appropriate, the principal must interact with the students to determine if the culmination of their task adequately meets the demand of the performance objective of the standard. When any of these links in the chain is missing, students are getting a lesser educational experience to some degree. In order for a principal to review all of these components, teachers must orient their planning around these skills. Teachers must have very clear expectations regarding how they will use and interact with these standards documents and make their content accessible to all.

If these are the expectations for teachers, principals must join them in this trench by being conversant on how the documents are laid out and what they mean. Principals themselves may not have the professional experience and mastery of the content to be able to design the best lessons using these documents.

However, they must practice and hone their skills to be able to follow along in an intelligent manner so it is clear that they can recognize whether what is supposed to be happening is, in fact, playing out through the course of the lesson. Further, independent of content-specific tasks, principals need to refresh their own learning on the varying levels of cognitive complexity. Becoming conversant on what recalling, defining, contrasting, predicting, and hypothesizing might look like, and how to recognize the difference between them is a prerequisite to being able to interact in a meaningful way with teachers regarding their instructional choices.

Closely related to an understanding of required state standards, the principal must also have a general understanding of the curriculum that individual teachers are supposed to follow to plan their instruction. Whether this is developed at a district level or whether individual building sites are able to define their curriculum, it is imperative that a principal ensure that the course of study is laid out in an organized and intelligent manner. One very important distinction that needs to be made is that the adopted materials and resources for a class are not synonymous with the curriculum for that class.

Despite constant efforts to instruct otherwise, educators continue to equate the adopted materials for a course with the actual curriculum for a course.

This is not only a mistake, but it can also lead to very serious problems within the classroom. Textbooks and accompanying resources certainly play an important role for teachers as they are a portion of the resources that will help a teacher operationalize the required standards as defined in their curriculum. However, it should be noted that resources are developed without any particular teacher in mind.

Because of the mass scale of textbook production, they are intended to be useful to as wide a variety of audiences as possible. This creates a situation where they are useful but do not necessarily fill the particular need of any given set of students. Indeed, individual state standards vary enough that the scope and sequence of a textbook may not necessarily encompass the depth and breadth of work that is required for a particular school.

A well-defined curriculum not only identifies state standards but works to prioritize those standards so that the most important and consequential standards are emphasized while other standards are used to support them. These prioritized standards are then thoughtfully laid out over the course of the school year with deliberation to ensure that standards play well together and are rolled out in a systematic fashion.

The curriculum is not sensible until it is laid out as a pacing guide for the teacher as well. This should not raise the concern that this forces teachers to follow a script. Pacing important work over the course of available instructional time is the only responsible way to plan for instruction. Time is a limited commodity and must be used thoughtfully. Without planning and pacing the curriculum over the course of the school year, leaders can never be sure that they have allocated adequate time for each piece of learning. When this is not done well, whatever learning that was supposed to happen at the end of the year is never taught. This leaves students at a distinct disadvantage as they transition into the next year's learning with a new teacher expecting that they know more than they ever learned during the prior year.

Despite the best efforts of textbook companies, textbooks will not necessarily match the obligations demanded by a district curriculum work. Historically, when teachers take their cue on what should be taught based upon a sequential ordering of the textbook, the only thing that can be guaranteed is that page sixteen is taught after page fifteen. Because the book orders it that way, it is taught that way. Most educators have had personal experience that the second half of their textbook is never used simply because the resource was too large and time ran out before they got to that section of the text.

In examining any text, it is quite clear that the authors did not put nonimportant information in the back half of the book. In fact, sometimes very critical pieces of learning reside in the last half of the book. The reason they are in the last half of the book is not because they are less important, but because something always has to be in the last half of a book. Usually, it is the most complex and demanding aspect of the course, and students are never exposed to this learning opportunity.

It is incumbent upon teachers to select only the portion of a textbook that assists them in meeting their current learning objectives as defined by a well-sequenced curriculum guide that is aligned with their adopted state standards. Principals must give teachers the permission to thoughtfully supplement and omit portions of textbooks and accompanying resources that do not assist them in meeting their current learning objectives. Many may object that this does not ensure fidelity in implementation. The truth is quite the opposite. Fidelity in the classroom should be focused upon the adopted curriculum, not the adopted resource.

The distinction is as simple as that between a blueprint for a house and the tools needed to construct the house. A builder would never state that the purpose of the day was to hammer. Indeed hammers will be used, but the point of the activity is not hammering, it is using the hammer to build the house that was designed in the blueprint beforehand. In the same way, the purpose of Tuesday is not page sixteen. The curriculum plan will likely include some portion of page sixteen to accomplish the underlying plan, but page sixteen is only a tool to meet a larger purpose. This revelation is difficult for many educators. While they quickly understand the analogy of hammer versus blueprints, they sometimes struggle to abide by it day by day within the classroom.

When teachers struggle to use their materials appropriately, it is usually for one of two reasons. The first is easier to remedy and is completely within the control of the principal. Sometimes, teachers believe that using materials page by page is actually the expectation. Delineating the difference between fidelity to the curriculum guide and the materials is all that is needed to address this situation. For these teachers, the clarification is very liberating. This approach gives teachers permission to skip over pages and sections of work if their students have already achieved mastery. There is nothing more demoralizing to a student than being forced to complete compliance work when they have already proven their competency.

Teachers are empowered to use their professional judgment to skip redundant or unnecessary sections when it is contrary to their established goals. It also gives them the flexibility to supplement with additional resources as necessary if students are still struggling. Indeed, page sixteen of the textbook may only supply five practice problems, and page seventeen covers a different topic. In this situation, teachers must recognize that their obligation to students extends beyond the five supplied problems and that their text is no longer a sufficient resource. This approach values the teacher as a decision maker and recognizes that teaching ends when learning occurs.

The other reason that teachers overrely on their resources is more difficult to unwind. Frankly, slogging through a textbook page by page is far easier on the teacher. This approach requires very little thought and planning. If students completed page sixteen on Tuesday, page seventeen becomes the default lesson plan for Wednesday. Kids deserve better. However, because page seventeen sounds math-ish, neither students nor parents see reason to object. The only way to refocus teachers who are falling into this thoughtless trap is by engaging them at the level of the standards-referenced learning objective rather than the resources or activity. Principals must intervene when the stated objective is "complete page sixteen" or "build a model rocket." Instead, leaders must demand that teachers describe the larger learning that will be accomplished during the day's class. This move forces a teacher to look beyond the book's table of contents and reframes learning by outcomes instead.

Educators are often quick to forget that the professional literature is replete with researched-based studies to determine what works best in classrooms. Both great and poor instructional practices are very well known. Despite this fact, poor practices remain deeply entrenched in the classroom, and sound instructional practices often do not have pride of place. Well-designed instruction is a combination of both the way in which a class is structured and the specific activities students are asked to complete around the chosen content.

In looking at anything a person learns throughout life, whether it be riding a bicycle as a child or learning to crochet as an adult, there is simply an inherent best approach to learning that resonates with human beings. Although it comes in many names and packages such as gradual release of responsibility and the workshop model, the transference of knowledge in a guided way from teacher to learner is key to great instruction. Obviously, the very reason a student is enrolled in a course is because they do know yet know the things that a student must know and be able to do.

Education places the more knowledgeable teacher in the role to bring the learner along in the process. Because of this, instruction must begin with a teacher modeling in both words and action what mastery of the objectives looks like. If it is a youngster teaching a sibling to ride a bicycle, the older sister begins by asking the sibling to "watch me do it." Modeling the expected skill with appropriate commentary is the beginning of the learning process. However, no one learned to ride a bike simply by watching others do it. Eventually, the teacher must cede some of the control and responsibility to the learner to begin performing the task. This is when the older sister steadies the handlebars with one hand while firmly holding the seat with the other. The younger learner is trying but still needs a lot of guidance and feedback in her attempt. This guided practice is this next critical aspect in sound instruction.

However, both siblings know that the whole point of learning to ride a bike is to be able to do it without a sister walking alongside. The learning is complete when the younger sister can independently complete the complicated sequence of steps needed to ride a bicycle. Teachers do not follow their students home at night. Students must develop a mastery of material independent from the assistance of their teacher. At this moment, the student has truly learned and the task is complete. The best teaching always includes teacher modeling, guided practice, and independent practice. While any given class period may not sensibly include every piece, some smaller tasks may be introduced, practiced, and brought to closure within the day. Regardless of the timing, each piece of this sequence is essential.

Independent from the way instruction is structured and organized, the actual instructional activities teachers require of their students matter greatly as well. Educational researchers have been warning for decades against the misuse of relentless lecturing, worksheets packets focused on keeping students busily compliant, and the detrimental effects of round-robin reading on fragile readers. These practices and many others must die a long-overdue death in classrooms. However, replacing these inferior practices with sensible and strong practices will not occur by accident. Indeed, it has not yet happened. Countless books and videos have been published highlighting the power of research-based instructional practices and are readily available. Examples such as Socratic seminars, graphic organizers, and think-pair-share are the tip of the proverbial iceberg when it comes to practices that connect students to learning. Principals must ensure that practices like these are the ways students spend their time in class.

However, a troubling phenomenon has emerged in classrooms with well-meaning teachers seeking to improve instruction. Teachers may attempt to include these great instructional techniques but implement them at the wrong time. When this happens, great practices become largely ineffective. Simply, most instructional practices are powerful *only when used in the proper context*. For example, asking students to share their thinking with a partner is an exercise in futility if the students have absolutely no background knowledge on the topic in question. The appropriateness of an approach is situational. There is indeed a place for interactive lecture, just as there is a place for a hands-on lab activity. However, equally important is the fact that there is a time when a lab activity would make no sense and would impede learning.

Principals must look deeper than the instructional activity to determine if a teacher is engaged in effective instruction. For example, suppose a principal entered a classroom and noticed that groups of students were gathered together working on a Venn diagram comparing and contrasting the causes of World Wars I and II. At first blush, the principal may be pleased that this corresponds to a strong learning target tied to an adopted state standard. Additionally, all students are actively engaged and this well-known instructional device to compare two distinct ideas is the method the teacher is using to capture student thinking. All is well. Or is it? The principal must dig a little deeper to see what the students are placing within the circles on the Venn diagram. Suppose that the wrong ideas were in the boxes. What is gained if the right strategy is used at the right time to cement the wrong thinking into students' minds?

Principals must acknowledge that this happens constantly in classrooms independent of the quality of the teacher. Students have missing knowledge and possess tremendous misconceptions on most every topic. Again, this is precisely because they are novice learners. If students had command of the nuances of the history of twentieth-century warfare, they would not need to be sitting in the very class where their misunderstandings are rearing their head. Obviously, this example is not meant to prove that the teacher had made a poor choice in the instructional approach. Rather, the teacher had a great start that needed a bit more attention before declaring it a success. Principals must help teachers understand that what they do as instructors certainly matters. Doing the right work and avoiding the wrong work are critical, but the work is not finished until the student learns. As the old joke goes, "I taught my dog to whistle. She didn't learn, but I taught her." The obligation to teach ends when the act of learning is complete.

The last aspect of teacher practice that needs examined is the way in which teachers assess student learning. Nothing seems to evoke as much criticism by both educators and the public as the strong opinion that students are being tested too much. This sweeping sentiment deserves further consideration. When educators claim that students are tested too much, do they mean the duration of one state exam is too long for their students? Or perhaps there are other required tests that they must administer that cause frustration. It is interesting to note that educators rarely pare back their own classroom-level testing despite this frustration. Have concerned educators scaled back classroom-level assessments in response to the testing movement? While educators must make thoughtful decisions about how much students need to be tested, the amount of testing can be controlled to a far greater degree than is often assumed. One way to determine if students are being tested appropriately is to analyze whether the results of any test are being used to make new instructional decisions for that student. The purpose of testing has a great deal to do with whether any given test is appropriate and useful.

Aside from high- or low-stakes summative testing that students are required to take, there is an entirely different form of assessment that must be regarded differently than formal exams. Formative assessment that is low stakes and ongoing is at the heart of great instructional practice. If the public is concerned with students spending too much time being tested, they should be equally concerned that teachers are not formatively assessing students enough.

Indeed, formative assessment should be constantly occurring in the classroom. This is not to say that this information should be bundled together and entered into the gradebook, but it absolutely should be used to inform and adapt instruction. Of course, teachers formatively assess students in a variety of ways. Whether it is an expression of confusion on a child's face or a more formal exit slip to assess understanding of students leaving the room, teachers have myriad of ways of checking for understanding throughout the classroom lesson.

Recognizing the importance of ongoing formative assessment is critical for a principal as they become involved in classrooms. Principals should be more alarmed when they don't see students being assessed than when they do. Again, this ongoing form of assessment does not always need to be memorialized in writing or recorded by the teacher, although this practice is often advisable. The appropriateness of assessment is as easily recognized as whether teachers have a constant handle on what students do and do not yet know and are making new decisions in light of that information.

Principals are able to determine whether this is happening in a number of ways. If principals notice teachers sitting at their own desks, they ought to pay close attention to what is actually happening. If a teacher is able to shift into that passive role, a principal should dig deeper and see what they are doing. When teachers have released students to work independently, they should not see this as an opportunity to shift to other tasks. Rather, these are the moments where teachers should be roaming the classroom to check on student progress. Whether it is clearing up a misconception or conferring with a student about their next steps, student independent work time presents one of the most powerful chances to improve student learning. Principals and teachers may be reluctant to interrupt students who are working quietly. However, unless teachers are assessing students in a meaningful way in these moments, students may be practicing and completing their work incorrectly.

Principals can easily get lost trying to concern themselves with too many things when conducting a classroom observation. Instructionally, there is one tactic that a principal can employ to focus many efforts on one aspect of an observation. Principals are able to discern much of what is happening by focusing on the questioning technique of the teacher. In examining the questioning technique of an educator, great insight on many other important areas are typically revealed. For example, a principal can ascertain information about a teacher's background knowledge on the subject matter based upon the questions that are asked. Likewise, principals can also see what amount of planning and preparation went into the lesson by observing the flow and thoughtfulness that goes into the questions the teacher asks of students.

Further, principals are also able to see the sort of engagement and rapport that teachers maintain with their students based upon the exchange of questions and answers during class. Obviously, principals are also able to see the manner in which teachers are informally assessing their students based upon the questions that are asked. Principals can also gain insight based on which students want to answer questions and which students teachers typically call on to answer questions during class. Master teachers are often far more interested in finding out why a student does not have their hand raised rather than affirming that a student with his hand raised knows the correct answer.

Additionally, principals are able to detect the cognitive depth of the classroom discussion based upon the questions a teacher is posing to students. It is important to remember the questions are not necessarily easy or hard based upon cognitive depth. For example, recall questions are very low in cognitive depth. This does not mean, however, they are always easy. For example, a student could be asked to recall Avogadro's number in a science classroom, and this may not be information that all students immediately are able to remember. This would be a very difficult, low-level question.

Likewise, questions of a high-cognitive depth are not always difficult. For example, a teacher could ask that same group of science students to hypothesize what would happen if a marble was rolled off a countertop. Hypothesizing requires a higher cognitive demand, but even small children will correctly predict that the marble will fall to the ground. Creating a hypothesis requires a higher cognitive demand than recall questions, but this hypothesis is certainly not more difficult than the recall-level question.

Principals and teachers need to work to understand that recall-level questions are not necessarily undesirable and questions that require a higher cognitive load are not always preferable. As with most things, it is entirely situational. There are times when a teacher most certainly wants to pepper the class with low-level recall questions to remind them where they left off by getting their bearings answering simple questions. This is entirely appropriate because it is thoughtful.

However, teachers should take great care to recognize when they rarely require anything more than low-level questions of their students. One specific strategy a principal can use is to script the actual questions that teachers ask students, students ask their teachers, and questions that students ask each other. Upon reviewing these questions at a later time with the teacher, principals can note both the quantity of questions asked during the timeframe and the quality of questions noting the various levels of cognitive complexity. Not only is this an objective way to review what actually happened within the classroom, but it also can assist teachers in future planning to ensure that teachers are thoughtfully planning and developing their questioning techniques. Quite simply, students cannot think critically if they are not being asked critical questions. This is an incredibly powerful method to gauge and improve instruction.

Typically, principals have received training in all aspects of quality classroom instruction that have been discussed thus far. However, each principal should reflect on the actual amount of academic preparation they received in curriculum and instruction to determine whether they have some gaps that need to be filled by seeking professional development for themself. Regardless, much of the focus of administrative preparation programs do not emphasize true instructional leadership. Therefore, even the most knowledgeable principals may need to spend some time refreshing their own knowledge base despite having a strong prior academic preparation program.

Principals should note that whatever form of preparation they received, whether through their own professional reading or formal coursework, the task for them is to implement this learning in very practical settings. The transition from theoretical to practical is not always easy. This commitment to instructional excellence is no longer focused on their own practices as a classroom teacher, but rather, it must be projected onto the teachers in their care. Principals must apply their own understanding of excellence in teaching that has been very personal to this point and apply it to all of their teaching faculty.

Obviously, this presents a number of challenges. Principals typically have expertise in one narrow curricular area where they were assigned as teachers themselves. The reality of their new task, however, is to apply the strong focus on fundamentals to a wide variety of classrooms and disciplines. Once again, the best approach is for principals to accept their own limitations and be readily transparent about them. If a principal formerly taught middle school science, one can easily imagine the lack of confidence a French teacher might have regarding their perception of how much of the teacher's content the principal actually understands. In fact, rather than being critical of the principal's lack of understanding, it is likely that the French teacher would not even have the expectation that the principal is able to engage in conversation about the discipline.

Taken to its logical conclusion, this presents a very disturbing possibility. Without efforts to bridge this gap, principals may find themselves in a position when their faculty do not believe they have the credibility to be conversant in any academic conversations except in the areas where the principal is certified. Principals would be making a gigantic mistake if they attempt to enter the world of other content teachers on equal footing by pretending to have commensurate skills in that discipline. Instead, principals must make extensive efforts to find enough common ground with all teachers that they do not resign themselves to irrelevancy and isolation from the majority of their faculty.

This should not be a source of stress or self-consciousness for a principal. The task is not to convince an honor's biology teacher that the principal has a comparative understanding of the discipline. To be a content expert in a wide variety of subjects and grade levels is impossible. In fact, even the most critical teachers would not expect that. Rather, the task of principals is to convince the teacher that they are interested and willing to engage in meaningful conversation about their discipline *despite* their own skill gaps. Humbly acknowledging ignorance is a powerful weapon for a principal in this moment. This admission of limitations, coupled with an acknowledgment of the teacher's expertise, is both encouraging for the teacher and a pleasant way to open the doors for further conversation. In fact, most teachers are greatly heartened to discover that their principal is both interested and willing to learn more about the expertise that they bring to their teaching. Embracing the knowledge gap in the content makes it much easier to provide commentary on the principal's observations about instructional strengths and weaknesses. This creates a partnership where both participants in the conversation are allowed to bring knowledge and expertise into the conversation.

Principals must seize this moment of seeming weakness and disadvantage and see it for the incredible opportunity that it is. When principals engage in difficult conversations humbly admitting their own ignorance, they are able to ask much more probing and pressing questions than might be possible otherwise. In this respect, principals are not being deceptive because they truly do not understand the particulars of why teachers are making the choices they are. However, when asked in a spirit of seeking to understand, very sensitive questions could be asked that might normally result in defensiveness by the teacher.

For example, if the principal with a background in mathematics is engaged in pointed conversations with a math teacher, the math teacher may be a bit defensive because he knows that the principal may have sufficient background skills and is actually questioning his competency. This is in contrast to conversations where a principal acknowledges personal skill gaps and asks deeply probing questions in the spirit of understanding rather than giving teachers the impression that their abilities are in doubt.

In these conversations, principals need to realize that they have the opportunity to capitalize on their own lack of understanding and begin relentlessly questioning the practices of the teacher in these ways. When done in the spirit of inquiry, even highly suspicious teachers will recognize that the principal is simply seeking to understand. Before principals are able to engage on the specific strengths and weaknesses of individual teachers, it is imperative that principals conduct a very comprehensive and thorough self-assessment of their own background knowledge, skills, and professional understanding of what great instructional practices look like.

Without this intimate level of reflection and willingness to build up their own knowledge base, principals will be ill-equipped to interact and engage with teachers in a consequential way. It is only in matching objective observations of a classroom teacher's behaviors against mutually agreed-upon best practices that both the principal and the teacher can get their bearings on what is actually happening, what should happen next, and how they should feel about that status.

Not only is it a gentle way for principals and teachers to openly discuss any shortcomings, but it also will likely identify areas of strength that should be cause for celebration. When these conversations are managed correctly, everyone involved can have a better picture of both the current lived experiences of students and the areas where their academic experiences can be improved.

Chapter 4

Identifying the Problems

In the medical profession, physicians are obliged to ensure at all times that their actions adhere to an accepted standard of care. This dictates the appropriate range of responses they are able to provide in every possible situation. In fact, when patients have a negative outcome while under a doctor's care, the first question that is asked is whether the treatment the patient received met the standard of care. Educators would benefit from seeing their profession in the same light. While the decisions educators make do not necessarily come at the price of life or limb, the stakes are very high for students. When principals begin difficult or critical professional dialogue with teachers, it is helpful to frame the conversation within the context of which practices fall within the educators' standard of care.

Principals are called to own the instructional conversation in their buildings. It is quite common to hear others urging someone to show commitment to an issue by demanding that they "own the problem," but it is easy to gloss over what it truly means to *own* an issue. Perhaps the best way to appreciate the true meaning is to contrast it with similar alternatives. Young people often are forced to rent the place where they live long before they ever buy a home. Anyone who has been in the real estate business knows that it is easy to tell the difference between a home that was rented and one where the residents were owners. Rented houses show characteristics of neglect and avoidance of issues both small and large. In fact many of the problems persist for so long that small issues become larger ones.

This is in stark contrast to the way most people view the home that they own. Not only do homeowners take great pride in preserving their home, but also they often take great steps to improve upon the conditions. Homeowners are not content to accept inferior conditions. Rather, they take active measures to make the best out of their present situation. This analogy holds true for a principal's role in classroom instruction as well. If principals are called to own the status of instruction in their buildings, they do not accept the status quo and certainly do not allow the quality of instruction to slowly deteriorate over time. They too are called to make improvements both major and minor to whatever conditions currently exist.

The principal who is committed to this work now stands at a crossroads. Up to now, if a leader has embraced the recommendations to commit to a true presence within classrooms and is willing to do so in an objective and nonjudgmental way, that leader must now make a decision. The leader has evaluated and improved any lagging skill sets that would keep him from entering into a professional conversation with credibility and must now make a decision to act. This decision to act will come at a price. Every decision to act and every decision not to act come at a price. It would be foolish to suggest that engaging in critical and crucial conversations with educators about their abilities as a professional is easy. It is never easy, but it is absolutely necessary. This can cause principals to shy away from the moment that is building.

There is no doubt that it is easier to avoid difficult conversations than to have them. That is true at least in the short term. However, principals must take the long view of this crossroads moment and be very clear about what is truly at stake. The quality of the existing relationship with the teacher is at a critical juncture where it may become defined in a brand new way. This can make principals hesitate at a crucial moment and choose to avoid necessary conversations. In these moments, principals feel that it is more difficult to say what needs to be said than to risk the fall-out of the way in which the relationship may change.

Typically, the only way that leaders can muster the conviction to engage in these sorts of conversations is to step back and consider what is truly at stake. Leaders must recognize that there is far more at risk than just the quality and status of their current relationship with other adults in the building. If the principal has decided that a classroom observation is troubling enough that a conversation is in order, the principal must also recognize that the impact of the troubling instructional behavior is being felt most by the students who live it.

Principals must keep in mind that students are a captive audience. They did not choose to be sitting in their assigned desks. The adults around them decided which room they would sit in and which teacher would take care of them. In these moments, principals must remind themselves that the questionable classroom practices are not occurring in a vacuum. They are playing out in the presence of children daily. In fact, principals must acknowledge that, for some children, the only educational experience they are receiving is from a teacher engaging in subpar practices.

Usually, principals are no strangers to volatile conversations with emotionally distraught students and parents. Often, these conversations are emotionally taxing for principals. Principals may rightfully feel like enough of their day is marked by controversy and confrontation with those they may not know very well and wonder if picking what could be perceived as a fight with a faculty member even makes sense in the larger scheme of things. Again, a fair response to this concern is that the conversation need not be seen as negative, and a principal must squarely address the price to be paid for not having the conversation.

One way for a principal to bring this reality to a gritty and visceral head is to engage in the following exercise. In the moment that the leader is feeling reluctant to engage with a teacher on questionable practices, the principal should envision the most struggling student in the class. The principal must vividly imagine walking up to the student, noticing their slumped shoulders and downcast demeanor, and say, "William, I know you are really struggling in Mr. Webber's class. I know you aren't a big fan of the way he just gives you worksheet packets every day and it isn't helping your understanding of the subject. I was thinking of talking to him about it, but I have chosen not to because I am worried that he won't be very happy with me. I'm deciding to do nothing instead."

Obviously, no principal would relish this kind of conversation with a struggling young person. Make no mistake about it, though. Every classroom has a William in it who is losing hope every day because the teaching methods aren't reaching him. William deserves better. William deserves a voice. William deserves a leader who will speak on his behalf.

Principals must also recognize that teachers may indeed choose to process the conversation in a negative way. That is not to say, however, that the principal must or should begin this conversation in any way that questions the dignity or integrity of the teacher. In fact, the principal should do the exact opposite. Leaders should always presume positive intent when beginning these difficult conversations with teachers.

There is no doubt that these conversations will be difficult. However, it does not mean that these conversations must be controversial or adversarial. In an age where people often voice their opinion in a less than civil manner, principals must possess the courage and the will to engage in a discourse that is rooted in respect and consideration for everybody concerned. Depending upon the approach they have taken thus far in their professional careers, this may not be a skill that has been well practiced.

Typically, principals are well practiced in maintaining their poise and demeanor when issues arise in their buildings. However, principals do not always have as much experience in initiating these conversations. When principals do initiate difficult conversations with personnel, it is likely regarding issues where a clear-cut violation of policy or procedure has been committed. As unfortunate as it may be, principals do get some practice in addressing issues such as repeatedly arriving to work late, failing to call back an angry parent, and failing to attend a mandatory meeting. While some principals may struggle with these conversations, even reluctant principals understand that these issues must be addressed. What is less clear is when teachers have not necessarily done anything wrong, but they may not be doing everything entirely right. These moments are hard enough to describe, let alone handle effectively.

Because educators often identify their very personhood with their job, it is especially difficult for some teachers to accept shortcomings they may have as a professional. Principals must be sensitive to this reality. Leaders must be reassured that there are ways to choose words wisely and keep these conversations healthy and productive. Words matter. Especially when the confidence and sense of identity may be at stake for a teacher, a principal must be very thoughtful in the way this conversation is held.

The first key to a productive conversation is the requirement that the principal must commit to a dialogue that is rooted in truth. This truth must be established by referring to actual events and behaviors that were witnessed firsthand. When a principal references the classroom with personal knowledge of what was observed, the conversation can stay focused on what indisputably happened. Describing these moments in concrete terms keeps the dialogue grounded in truth.

In these moments, principals must resist the urge to soften the blow by downplaying or dismissing the very problems they intended to discuss. This can often happen once the conversation has begun and the principal begins to sympathize if the teacher begins to react emotionally. If a principal believes an issue is worth addressing but then diminishes the importance of it after seeing the teacher's reaction, the teacher will likely be confused rather than relieved. Leaders must steel themselves in this moment to see the conversation through in truth. If students were sleeping during the lesson, a principal must say as much. If students were unable to complete the assignment because they were confused by the lecture, the principal must relay that information.

One way to keep the conversation rooted in truth and limit the tendency for it to become a battle of wills is for the leader to resist the urge to label behaviors. Principals must remember lessons that they learned after years of experience working with parents through difficult discipline situations. For example, if a student tells a teacher to shut up, a principal learns very quickly how to relay this information to a parent seeking to defend their child. A wise principal might say, "The teacher asked your son to sit down and your son said, 'Shut your fat mouth.' We will need to have a discipline hearing as this violates our school rule against disrespect."

As unhappy as the parent may be, there is not much to argue. A novice principal getting ready to learn a lesson the hard way might say, "We need to have a discipline hearing as your son was rude and disrespectful today in class." When phrased this way, the parents may decide they take exception to the label being placed on their child and begin arguing whether telling someone to shut up meets their operating definition of rude and disrespectful. The principal is better off accurately describing the behavior rather than defining what that behavior says about the child.

Likewise, principals must resist the tendency to label ineffective classroom teaching strategies as well. Teachers must accept the statement, "When I walked into your room while you were lecturing, seven students had their heads on the desk sleeping, and Justin was throwing wads of paper across the room." This statement is indisputable. Contrast that statement with the following, "When I walked into your room, no one was paying attention and it was chaotic."

Again, the principal must now convince the teacher that a student throwing paper meets the definition of a classroom in chaos. What is lost in those moments is a focus on the teacher's inattention to inappropriate behavior. Avoiding the tendency to label teacher behaviors is even more critical when there is not a glaring issue to be addressed like students sleeping, but rather an instructional decision that was inferior but hardly inappropriate.

When principals begin these conversations with teachers, they must remember that the initial task is to describe what was observed in a careful and accurate manner. They must take the time to discuss it openly, accepting the teacher's response throughout the description and clarifying and altering their words as the situation warrants. In this conversation, describing what was happening and how it falls short of best practices is entirely different and separate from *how the teacher should feel about it*. The principal should have no interest in eliciting an emotional reaction from the teacher in light of the conversation. Even if the teacher were to show remorse and apologize, agreeing with the principal's observation, this is not the point of the exchange.

The principal's intent should not be to be proven right. Moreover, the intent should not be to shame the teacher into feeling bad about it. Rather, the focus and outcome of the conversation is simply to describe what the principal witnessed, observe how it differs from the best accepted practice, and focus on the ways the principal can assist in bridging the approach to get closer to that instructional ideal.

In a similar way, principals must also avoid speaking in overgeneralizations and absolutes. When a leader claims that a teacher always does something, it is natural for the teacher to focus on the frequency of the behavior, trying to remember occasions when it did not happen, rather than keeping the focus on the times it did. In these conversational moments, exaggeration does not emphasize the problem; it distorts the problem. As clarity and accuracy are important, the principal's description of the problem cannot be distorted in this way.

Because of the delicate nature of the conversation and the many ways in which it can turn out poorly, it is imperative that the principal have the courage to meet in person with the teacher to visit. The perceived convenience and immediacy of e-mail is not appropriate for these conversations. Certainly, the principal wants to engage in this conversation in a timely manner. Describing an instructional problem and its urgency certainly loses its momentum if it is addressed weeks after the fact.

However, principals make a mistake by failing to communicate important matters in person. Some believe it is preferable because it creates a paper trail noting the problem. This notion must be immediately abandoned. If a principal feels the need to memorialize a concern, it must be a summary and description of the meeting to address the issue. The first time a teacher hears about a troubling aspect of their teaching, they deserve to look the principal in the eye when they hear it. This approach also ensures that the way in which the principal hoped to relay the concern is indeed the way the teacher is processing it. E-mail messages cannot begin to convey tone or emphasis that accentuates the truth that needs to be revealed. Rather, they only serve to put the teacher on notice of the general topic, and then imaginations run wild as a concerned teacher tries to parse out the meaning and implication of the principal's statements. If principals are concerned enough to want to discuss the matter, they must possess the will to engage in a personal conversation.

Principals often make the mistake of trying to hustle too quickly through this conversation. They should not see the goal as relaying information to the teacher at issue. Rather, this must be a conversation. Conversations go back and forth with everyone offering their perspective and reasons for their thoughts and actions. Often, this conversation will reveal unknown bits of information that cast the concern in a new light. The principal should certainly steer the conversation to a place where it remains on topic but must also know that sometimes teachers have reasons behind their choices that are not readily apparent. There is, after all, a difference between a reason and an excuse. Principals must listen carefully to distinguish between the two as the story is fleshed out.

The very nature of this conversation is likely to elicit an emotional reaction from the teacher even if that is not the desired outcome. This is quite natural. Teachers care deeply about their work even on occasions where they are not masters at it. Likewise, everyone is forced to take a deep breath when a superior is critical of their work. Principals must manage the conversation carefully to ensure that it does not transform from its original intent.

A conversation that begins around a lack of teacher preparation of the day's lesson can easily devolve into one where the principal ends up only managing the emotion that is brought to the surface when it is addressed. Sadness is not the only emotion that may come to the surface, however. In these moments, teachers will often become angry and resentful. Principals must stay poised and not allow their own emotions to surface in response. When a teacher responds to a principal's concerns in anger, the principal will lose the chance at having a productive conversation if the anger is countered by indignation at a subordinate responding negatively.

If the leader successfully keeps their emotions in check, they need to remember that stifling the teacher's emotional response is not the point of the meeting either. Principals should be supportive and empathetic at the emotion that emerges but keep the conversation professional and on point. The only time a principal should reconsider the emotion that is evoked is if the emotion seems to be supported by more information that would suggest the principal's observation was somehow inaccurate. A teacher may feel resentful of the conversation if the classroom observation was incomplete or misunderstood. However, a teacher may also feel resentful if the principal simply has the nerve to question the classroom instructional decisions. One sort of resentment should bother the principal and challenge them to rethink their assessment of what is happening in the classroom. Living with the other sort of resentment is part of the burden a true leader must carry.

Once the principal commits to engage in critical conversations with teachers, the principal may very well wonder where to begin. In a building serving hundreds of students with many employees, there are countless combinations of behaviors and actions that may require attention. Many of the activities and approaches are highly commendable and deserve considerable attention. However, at this point, the principal must first clean up and address disturbing actions.

Principals may have a difficult time deciding where to begin. Obviously, issues regarding student welfare and safety are entirely different circumstances that demand serious and immediate attention. Aside from these crisis moments, principals must make decisions to determine which instances and topics should be addressed. The proper order of action is an important consideration as well. Deciding which teachers to visit with first and which ones can wait requires thoughtful consideration. Principals do not always have the luxury of shutting off the flow of urgent matters to give careful consideration to the most important issues in their building. However, principals must interrupt this natural flow and do this exact sort of planning.

A principal can become totally consumed with reactive managerial tasks rather than proactive leadership tasks. An effective leader must give preference and attention to important instructional matters. For example, when a principal receives a phone call from an angry parent complaining about a teacher's late work policy, this could easily become the total focus of the principal's next scheduled conversation with the teacher. Suppose that the principal also has significant concerns about the teacher's lack of engagement strategies with reluctant learners. Engaging reluctant learners is an important issue that affects many kids. Addressing the parent complaint is certainly necessary but may not even be a truly objectionable practice. Being upset does not necessarily mean the parent is right. Without a thoughtful plan, the principal may indeed focus on the immediacy of the parent concern and leave the engagement issue unaddressed. The urgent cannot eclipse the important.

Principals may find that even if they focus on the truly important matters within their school, there still remains a whole host of issues that need to be addressed. Within important matters, principals are still able to prioritize which items to address in a thoughtful way. By reviewing the way teachers instruct within a class lesson, principals can begin to see that some behaviors have higher leverage in ensuring success than others. For example, if an administrator were to observe problems in the way a teacher puts together the planning for a lesson and also struggles with managing classroom procedures, it may appear that there are two distinct issues requiring attention.

However, upon further consideration, the principal may reasonably conclude that the poor planning for instruction made it nearly impossible for the teacher to later manage classroom procedures and transitions between activities. Trying to problem solve poor procedures is likely to be fruitless without considering the teacher's poor structure in preparation and planning. The principal could conclude that better preparation is a behavior with higher leverage in making for a successful lesson. Addressing classroom procedures would not be possible without also attending to the poor preparation. However, first attending to the poor planning may, in fact, improve planning and fix many of the problems in managing procedures along the way. Even if the procedures are not completely ironed out, it is likely to be a much easier issue to improve afterward. Examining the breadth of problems observed can often result in a principal discovering a causal chain of problems that are cascading out from a high-leverage source.

In fact, teachers often appear to have multiple classroom deficiencies when one larger issue is manifesting as another. Much like a virus that manifests as a fever, the symptom is really not the real problem that needs to be addressed. For example, suppose that Principal Wagner and a teacher enter into the following discussion.

Teacher: "Was everything okay today when you came into my class?"

Principal: "I was just stopping by to debrief with you on that topic if you have a few minutes."

Teacher: "Well, I'm sure you saw that some kids weren't doing anything during their work time."

Principal: "I walked in about five minutes into the class. What did I miss?"

Teacher: "They were working on the packet for unit two from the beginning of class so what you saw when you walked in was about it."

Principal: "Tell me a bit about the packet. It looked like prepackaged materials."

Teacher: "Yeah, it is from our old textbook series, but I've always liked it so we still use it."

Principal: "James told me that some of the questions are impossible because the books don't match and they can't find the answers to some of them."

Teacher: "They are not impossible. James is a good example of the laziness I'm dealing with. I cannot get him engaged. Or some of the others."

Principal: "When I first walked in, I counted three students with their heads on their desk and four others visiting quietly."

Teacher: "Like I said, their lack of engagement is becoming a real problem."

This principal has done a number of things well thus far. In a timely way, Principal Wagner stopped by to debrief about the lesson. The concern she had regarding the lesson is fresh in everyone's mind and met face to face to talk further about it. Further, she also acknowledged that she missed the first few minutes of class and inquired if there was something that would have added to the context of the discussion. The teacher begins to offer explanation of the students' lack of engagement in the day's assignment, labeling the students as both disengaged and lazy. The principal continues to be objective in the observation clearly noting how many students exactly were having problems with the assignment.

When the conversation turned to the worksheet packet, the teacher wanted to skirt the issue of the quality of the assignment and focus instead on the students' behavior. As they continue talking, the principal has an opportunity to focus the issue on the weak assignment. The principal must reframe the teacher's conclusion that engagement is the problem when, in fact, the worksheet packet is the true issue that needs to be addressed.

Through a thoughtful conversation, the principal must help the teacher understand that students will not be highly engaged in a weak activity. When the teacher improves the instruction, the engagement should come along with it. In this scenario, the teacher gave outdated worksheet packets to students and expected them to be on task and engaged while answering fill-in-the-blank questions. The teacher must first ensure his instruction is anchored in engaging and effective practices before the issue can be accurately identified as simply poor student engagement. Without controlling the variable of great instruction, the principal cannot allow the teacher to label students as the problem. Adults and students alike flinch at the prospect of doing meaningless work.

Principals must also recognize that even an open-minded teacher focused on professional growth and development may not be able to handle deep conversations on a multitude of problems. This can become overwhelming and disconcerting, causing the teacher to shut down. Principals should view this work much like a physician trying to bring healing to a wound. The deepest problems must be addressed, letting the healing work from the inside out. Setting aside superficial items ensures that the most important behaviors are being addressed and corrected and also sends a strong message that the principal is not nitpicking in their involvement with teachers. Leaders must realize that complex problems take time to resolve if done properly. Teachers will need support and practice in approaching their work in a better way. Overwhelming teachers with many behaviors to adjust is likely to result in superficial changes that are not deeply rooted in lasting effect.

This thoughtful prioritization of which concerns to address at the beginning is in no way lowering standards for performance that principals expect from teachers. Rather, their guidance is focused on consequential matters first. This is not acceptance of inferior instruction or leniency in addressing concerns. It is a structured approach to remedying problems in a consistent and precise manner.

Principals need to remain mindful that even teachers who struggle greatly in the classroom may have many strong qualities as well. It is doubtful that a principal will work with a teacher who has no redeeming qualities. In fact, many teachers who lack skills in one instructional area may be rather strong in another aspect. Not only is this important to consider in keeping a balanced and fair opinion of other educators, but there is also an opportunity hidden within this fact upon which a principal may capitalize. Because all aspects of teaching are interwoven inextricably with each other, each component has an effect on all others. In one regard, this can certainly present a complicating factor to instruction as one area can negatively affect other areas.

Trying to decide which area of instructional weakness is the culprit causing the most immediate and negative impact is as challenging as unweaving threads from a piece of cloth. However, this also works to the benefit of the leader. If the principal takes the time to determine which areas of instruction are strong points for the teacher, the principal can use it as a strong outpost from which to add strength to weaker areas. Consider the following scenario between a young principal and her professional mentor:

Principal: "Thanks for thinking through this problem I'm having with Ms. Carerra. She is really frustrating me."

Mentor: "What's going on?"

Principal: "Well, I have had her on a plan of improvement on three different occasions for some instructional issues."

Mentor: "You didn't move to terminate her?"

Principal: "No, I genuinely want her to get better. She does get better in some ways for short periods of time. But it is like she fulfills exactly the demands of the plan of improvement but doesn't internalize the change and make it a part of how she teaches."

Mentor: "Which areas are troubling you?"

Principal: "I don't feel like she is well prepared for the lesson. Her classroom management and procedures are often scattered. Her only saving grace is that kids like her."

Mentor: "Like a buddy?"

Principal: "No, not at all. It's actually quite endearing. If I had to describe it, I'd say they see her as a mother figure. In fact, I was in there the other day and she was quietly conferring with David. He's this giant kid who is always in a bit of trouble. You'd think that he'd run all over her, but they were talking about his struggles with the lesson, much like if a parent were helping their child around the dinner table."

Mentor: "Well, that's pretty good, right?"

Principal: "Yeah, but it was like low-level chaos on the other side of the room. Again, nothing terrible because they kind of like her, but not well engaged either."

Mentor: "Maybe you can build off of that?"

Principal: "How do you mean?"

Mentor: "Does she like engaging in those quiet conferring sessions with kids?"

Principal: "Yeah, in fact, she has told me that's what keeps her holding on."

Mentor: "Does she disagree with you about needing to be better prepared in her lesson planning?"

Principal: "Not at all. She just says she's not very focused on it."

Mentor: "There's the answer. You have to help her see that she is only able to do the part she likes best, if she manages the rest to a degree that it doesn't interrupt the good stuff. Connect the two."

Rather than seeing these two skill sets as being separate and distinct areas of performance, the mentor sees the opportunity to connect the strong attribute to the weaker one in a way to coax better performance. If the teacher truly values conferring with students, certainly the principal could begin to identify specific occasions when this teacher was not able to do the thing she loved most because she was constantly redirecting off-task behavior. Seeing the need to shore up weaknesses in order to preserve and enhance the portion of the instruction that was both strong and important provides a powerful anchor for the principal to set future expectations. This teacher theoretically understood the importance of managing classroom procedures but hadn't committed to ensuring its sound functioning in the classroom. Perhaps linking the very possibility of genuine conferring sessions with students to the amount of lost instructional time is the best chance to focus new attention to these lagging areas of performance.

While much attention has been given to poor and weak instructional practices, the principal must also recognize the potential that engaging in genuine instructional conversations has to improving instruction that is already very good. This work should not be limited only to performance so low that it is troubling. Teachers perform across an entire educational spectrum. This work has great potential for teachers who desire to get even better at areas of their performance no matter how strong it is.

In the following exchange, a high school English teacher has asked a principal to come observe a writing lesson and offer some feedback on its success.

Teacher: "What did you think of the writing activity today?"

Principal: "Well, let me tell you what I think I observed. You had a writing prompt on the board that the students wrote about for nearly fifteen minutes, then they exchanged papers with a peer and they each edited the other's paper providing a critique of what they read."

Teacher: "Yes. Something is just not right, though. The students were highly engaged in both the writing and the peer editing, but their writing is just not very good."

Principal: "Were the students finding the errors that their peers had made?"

Teacher: "Yes, but truthfully there aren't really that many errors. They aren't making mistakes, but their writing just isn't very sophisticated."

Principal: "Describe how it is unsophisticated. What is missing?"

Teacher: "Well, look at this one. He only made a few small grammatical errors and his partner found those. But look, he writes mostly in simple sentences, low vocabulary, and only uses simple grammatical devices."

Principal: "Did your directions require that they use more advanced vocabulary or complex sentence construction?"

Teacher: "No, the directions didn't require any of that. But I have taught them those things, and they have shown that they understand how to use them on different assignments."

Principal: "Well, perhaps they do know how to write in a more sophisticated way but lack the confidence or willingness to do so. Couldn't you require them to incorporate them in their response?"

Teacher: "Yeah, I could give them the prompt and within the directions make sure that they use a number of related vocabulary terms, include three to five compound and complex sentences, and use whichever grammatical devices we are working on at the moment."

Principal: "That sounds like a reasonable expectation. If you hope to see it in their writing, you must require it. You might also ask them to highlight the portion of their response where they incorporated them. They could highlight vocabulary in yellow, complex sentences in green, and so on."

Teacher: "Yes! That would cue them to verify that they've met the expectation, and it would also make it much easier for me to notice when grading them as well."

At this point, the principal is revealing a whole new layer of instructional possibility for the teacher to consider. The teacher thus far has done a fine job of requiring a challenging writing prompt from her students and has added the strong instructional approach of peer editing to the classroom expectations. This is a very strong start. It is important to note that the teacher has not done anything wrong.

However, the principal has an incredible opportunity to take the instruction to an entirely different level. As the conversation progressed, the principal was able to suggest introducing more advanced vocabulary and sentence structure requirements into the writing process. No doubt, with these advanced expectations, students would begin writing in more sophisticated ways. Additionally, in the peer editing process, peers would start to identify more errors as students begin using structures and conventions that they had shied away from up to this point. The teacher can easily increase this level of rigor while still offering appropriate instructional support so that they find success with these new expectations and do not simply make more errors.

Helping students develop sophistication in their writing is difficult. The complexity of the work is compounded when students are reluctant to express themselves in their writing with conventions that are beyond their comfort level. This phenomenon leaves teachers with little raw material to refine. Thus, a teacher's opinion of what kids are able to do is often skewed by how willing they are to expose their weaknesses. However, much like a novice musician, their best efforts are currently only going to resemble the repetitious basics they have rehearsed. Truly creative work is often possible only by conscientiously stepping out of a comfortable framework.

Teachers must explicitly lead this effort by requiring nonmastered skills to be used in their students' written work. Without requiring them to stretch themselves academically, many students are not likely to push themselves into deeper levels of sophistication. In this scenario, the teacher was on the cusp of transforming the classroom experience in a powerful way. The principal's nudge is often the only catalyst the teacher needs to find a new type of instructional success.

Principals may gain great insight into the next steps they must take by asking the teacher to reflect upon why they are doing what they are doing and why they appear to be getting the results that they are. Oftentimes, teachers make decisions that feel right but are not accompanied by thoughtful reflection that can reveal very interesting information. Principals need to ask the question in order to gain additional information that can be helpful in taking next steps.

For example, principals should ask the question, "Can you please help me understand . . . " This question is a nonaccusatory way of asking teachers to explain a decision they have made. This question usually prevents teachers from becoming defensive because the leader is not focusing the question on why they did what they did as if they could be wrong. Rather, the question focuses on helping the principal understand why they took a particular approach. There is a subtle nuance that keeps the conversation both positive and focused on explaining the thinking behind an instructional choice. This statement alone can add tremendous insight into the "why" behind a choice. If the reasons behind the choice make good sense, it can reveal that the behavior is what needs attention. If the principal is troubled with the reason why the teacher made the decision, the conversation can focus there instead.

The principal can also ask the question, "What is your theory on why this is happening?" This is a powerful question to ask teachers when a phenomenon is observed. Not only does it add a layer of trust in valuing the teacher's opinion, but it also reinforces the notion that there are underlying reasons why certain results are obtained. This question seeks to get teachers to focus on the reasons why things happen as they do. Closely associated, another question that can be used is, "To what do you attribute this result?" Again, this helps connect observable results with reasons why it may be happening. The difference with this question is that it seeks more immediate causes rather than a complete underlying theory on why something is happening. Depending on the nature of the issue at hand, either question may be more appropriate.

With these actions, the principal is seeking to venture into deep thinking with a teacher. Some ideas and behaviors are superficial in nature. For example, the decision to have students work with a partner rather than a small group is a simple decision. The teacher probably put some level of thought into the decision, but it did not require deep reflection. Principals must differentiate between moments that do not need deeper analysis and the kinds of attitudes and behaviors that warrant deeper probing and investigation. Some questions have deep answers at their core.

Principals must take caution in what they accept as a sufficient answer to the probing questions they ask of their teachers. Often, when teachers attempt to explain a problem, they actually cite another problem as the answer. For example, suppose a principal were to ask a teacher what his theory is on the steep decline of student performance on a recent district-level assessment. If the teacher were to hypothesize it was due to poor student attendance, the principal may accept that as an answer. Simply knowing that attendance is to blame will not result in student performance increasing in the future without future actions. While poor attendance is the reason for the problem of poor grades, poor attendance is now a more fundamental problem that needs to be addressed.

Principals must maintain focus in these conversations to reframe the problem as new suggestions are offered. This ensures that the final explanation for the root of a problem is something that can then be addressed and solved. Suggesting that attendance is the reason for poor test results should trigger the principal into looking deeper into the attendance at the school. The principal could then determine if absences are correlating with low test scores. Simply accepting attendance as the reason for low test scores is to suggest a new problem is the solution. Principals cannot accept this as the end of the conversation. Rather, it is instead the recognition of a new problem that needs to be addressed.

Likewise, some problem-solving sessions end up becoming an exercise in explaining the problem in greater depth rather than working to a solution. For example, if the principal in the aforementioned example sought further information about the underlying reasons for the lower test scores, the teacher may continue to elaborate by noting that the girls in the class did better than the boys and that students in poverty performed the worst on the exam.

Although this is interesting information that may begin to shed light on which students need more interventions, it does little to offer a potential solution. In response, a principal should ask what the teacher would suggest that should be done to respond to the poor performance of certain groups. Often, educators become intrigued by additional insights describing a problem and forget that the additional information may isolate the problem to a particular group in a way that had not been previously understood. However, this new information does not yet offer a potential solution. Principals must encourage these insights but remain engaged in getting to the root of each problem, and then focus on potential solutions for each.

When principals engage in difficult instructional conversations that are solution-focused, teachers are often reluctant to accept new ideas as potential solutions. This reluctance can be for a number of reasons. Sometimes, teachers are simply hesitant to dismantle former practices and take the time to learn a more effective approach. For others, there is a common hesitancy to embrace a new solution that is not perfect.

For example, if a principal observed that a science teacher spent an inordinate amount of time lecturing to students and gave very little opportunities to experiment with lab activities, a principal may rightly decide to discuss this with the teacher. A reluctant science teacher may object, noting that the science budget is not sufficient to conduct numerous labs and that some of the students' behavior could make the classroom unsafe. Is the teacher correct?

Perhaps both objections are true to some extent, but the proposed solution of engaging in more hands-on activities is a much better solution than the current approach even if it comes with some added difficulties. Principals must guard against the tendency to look for the faults in new ideas. While not perfect, the new solutions are often less problematic than the current problem. Principals must acknowledge that the problems will not be ignored and that everyone needs to work together to work out the kinks associated with the new solutions. However, a chronic problem will not be allowed to persist simply because proposed solutions are not perfect.

At this point, principals need to step back from the particulars of each staff member and their observed strengths and weaknesses and take stock of the current educational landscape. Principals need to begin to develop a new narrative for the reality of their learning environment. Typically, educators develop a narrative to explain the reality around them. Unfortunately, the stories that are told are often speculative at best. In order to make sense of complex social dynamics, educators try to bring coherence out of the chaos by creating a narrative to summarize what is happening. Often, this is based on far too little observable data and the principal fills in the gaps with generalization and incomplete hypotheses.

For example, a principal might note that their school has a very high mobility rate and lagging test scores. It would be easy to begin weaving a story together that paints a picture that the low test scores are due to the high rate of mobility within the district. Obviously, the principal must move beyond anecdotes. A number of questions are in order before a story can be told. Are kids mobile for different reasons? Are some kids mobile due to poverty while others are mobile due to special programs offered at other schools? Are the test scores of the mobile students lower in a statistically significant way? Do mobile students have other confounding variables (like poverty) in their lives that may have more to do with their performance than being mobile? It is far too early to begin concocting a story to explain the reality of this school.

Unfortunately, many people in the environment do not wait for all of the facts to begin creating the narrative to explain events. Principals must be diligent in listening for the stories that are told. They must write them down and begin filling in the actual evidence that would either support or refute them. People have a relentless need to bring order to their environment. It is too unpredictable to exist in a complex setting without the ability to describe the pattern for why things happen the way they do. This, however, can be very dangerous because educators often begin to make very important decisions for students in light of the stories they believe to be true. The following is an actual account of principal's close call with allowing an inaccurate story to become the truth of the building:

Teacher: "Are you going to merge the recent state exam scores with each of our individual class rosters?"

Principal: "Yes, I'm actually almost done. It's a bit frustrating though because I have to merge two spreadsheets. One has the exam scores and the other has your roster of kids. It just takes a while because there are so many kids and teachers."

Teacher: "I hate to be a bother, but I am very anxious to get mine. Can you put mine together while I wait?"

Principal: "Sure, but go slow as I haven't double-checked my work."

(Later that day)

Teacher: "We need to talk about my test scores. My honor's algebra students did very poorly. I'm so upset. But as I think more about it, they are a lower class than past year. I think we have made a mistake advancing so many kids at an early age. They come to me with all sorts of gaps. I think we need to meet with the junior high teachers and rethink the way we pipeline students into honor's courses."

Principal: "Mr. Johnson, I am so sorry. I was in such a hurry to get you your data that I made a mistake when I merged the data. Every student's score was off by one row. I have fixed it, but everything I gave you was wrong."

Teacher: "How did my honor's class actually do?"

Principal: "Top scores in the district. . . . "

Not only is this true story a reality check for the importance of producing accurate data for teachers, but it is also a powerful lesson of how stories get written. It has been said that there are two ways to shoot a bull's eye in archery. One way is to aim carefully. The other way is to shoot randomly and paint the bull's eye around whatever spot the arrow landed. This second way is emblematic of the way educators often develop stories to support whatever result is obtained. It is easy to imagine how quickly an entire district's approach to teaching mathematics could have been unraveled had the story based on inaccurate data been allowed to persist.

Principals must engage in relentless questioning of everything that is believed to be true. If a theory exists, it must be supported by actual observable data. With humility, principals must acknowledge that preconceived notions about the very fundamentals of the school may be inaccurate. Principals can engage in this relentless questioning in a way that does not seem suspicious or off-putting. One technique a principal can ask to determine the likelihood of a prevailing opinion is to simply ask, "How do we know that is true?" When a teacher responds with anecdotal evidence to support the narrative, a principal can follow with, "To what extent might it be true? Who isn't it true for?" These questions gently probe the boundaries of truth in the stories that are told and clearly define when a peer may be over generalizing the state of affairs.

Developing a culture where it is expected that leaders rewrite the narrative of reality must become commonplace. Acknowledging assumptions and untested theories must become a part of the way educators hold each other accountable in discussing next steps. In time, educators will not feel like they are being questioned by suspicious coworkers. Rather, the culture of the building will instead value a relentless search for explanations that are rooted in truth and experience. This, of course, demands that educators focus their efforts on what actions and behaviors trigger the best results.

Principals must have the courage to address practices that are ineffective. Further, principals must have the wisdom and insight to assist willing teachers who seek to improve their solid practices. However, principals will soon find themselves in a quandary where multiple opinions are being offered and many of them may seem equally reasonable. In these moments, how does a principal respond?

Teachers often have very strong philosophical belief systems regarding the best way to teach their students. These strong opinions can often grind the work of a building to a halt if the educators believe that their approach is mutually exclusive to all others. Many teachers truly believe they have the market cornered on how to teach and pressure their peers greatly to adapt to their ways. Historically, principals have adopted a "live and let live" approach to these educational log jams. As a result, the instructional approach can vary greatly from one classroom to the next. It could be argued that siblings often receive entirely different educations while only separated by a thin classroom wall. Being stuck at these educational crossroads can be very unnerving for a principal.

Principals must embrace a very straightforward response to the moments where teachers are vying for their approach to be validated apart from all others. In this moment, the principal should say, "I appreciate the passion in your beliefs. Of course, others have equally strong opinions coming from a different philosophical approach. Here's what we need to do. The ultimate purpose for everything we do is to ensure that students learn at the highest levels possible. Please identify the assessment that will measure the learning for this issue. To begin, I will support every instructional approach that seems rooted in acceptable practice. If your approach is superior, students will learn at higher levels. Let's reconvene when the results are in to determine next steps."

This approach immediately cuts through theoretical clutter and gets to the heart of the matter. Student learning trumps everything. If teachers do indeed have a superior approach, it will be proven by results. In turn, principals must be prepared to press teachers into adopting new practices in light of any subpar results. This tactic cuts through complex and passionate philosophical debate and forces the adults to judge the worth of their practices by examining student work product. Not only is this a true way to resolve timeless debates among staff, it recenters the adults on the critical importance of student learning. Student learning must be the constant measuring stick for all decisions.

Chapter 5

Nurturing Untapped Potential

Principals who commit to improvement efforts in their school are true instructional leaders. The most impactful way to improve student achievement is by improving the quality of instruction delivered by teachers. Leaders must search the skill sets of their teachers and work to uncover the great potential that lies just below the surface. To successfully tap into this greatness, a principal may simply need to encourage a teacher to develop an already competent skill to a higher level of excellence. It may also require coaching a teacher to end an ineffective practice in exchange for a proven method of instruction.

Great leaders recognize that stakes are high for students, and a successful classroom experience goes far beyond student satisfaction and comfort in the moment if educators are to maximize academic potential. Students need excellent instruction in order to master the level of rigor that is expected of a student in the twenty-first century. This need is exacerbated for students who struggle and depend heavily upon their teacher to bridge their learning gaps and difficulties. Principals are tasked with ensuring each learner receives the quality of instruction necessary to accelerate growth and achieve success. They must also attend to instructional shortcomings that have immediate and negative effects on students. Problems of this sort cannot be denied or delayed in addressing.

In the midst of this challenging work, principals must resist the urge to view their teachers through a deficit lens. Teachers exhibiting weak instructional practices are not necessarily bad teachers, and they certainly are not likely to be bad people. Principals must guard against developing negative attitudes regarding the very people who are making students their life's work. Principals must reject negative behaviors but must embrace their people and hold them in a positive and hopeful light.

A physician assisting an athlete with a shoulder injury does not focus exclusively on the injured limb. The doctor examines the athlete and notes that an otherwise healthy person stands before them and has a separated shoulder. The separated shoulder does not define everything about the athlete, but the separated shoulder is indeed impacting the athlete's body from functioning at full strength. It may also be limiting the athlete's other body parts from functioning properly as well.

Similarly, a teacher engaged in weak instruction remains a dedicated professional who currently has a weak aspect to his functioning that is limiting his ability to perform at full potential. The principal must adopt the positive outlook of the physician and look with optimism at the potential of those in front of them. Teachers have a keen sense of whether a leader believes in them. Leaders cannot give an appearance of pessimism or cynicism when engaging in difficult conversations. A pessimistic attitude presumes that the current level of performance is a permanent condition.

Why would a principal even bother engaging in conversation if the behavior were inevitable? Approaching a teacher with a pessimistic attitude is to negate the entire growth-based mindset that is the foundation of teaching. As an educator, principals must have an unflagging belief that learning is inevitable in the hands of a great teacher. If this belief is true for students as learners, it is true for teachers as learners as well.

It would be wise for a principal to recognize that despite the numerous problems they must address, there are many positive qualities in each of the people with whom they work. People are truly complex, and the negative behaviors they are addressing are merely one small aspect of an otherwise positive and helpful person. When the principal embraces the fact that people are generally good and couples this realization with how many of these good people exist in the educational setting, they should be incredibly encouraged at the numerous positive actions and interactions happening every minute in the building. Despite the difficulties encountered by the challenges of a multitude of social interactions, the reality of most schools is largely positive and healthy. In order to create the proper sense of balance and perspective, principals must pay special attention to all that is good in the school.

With every conversation principals begin, they make a substantial investment. Primarily, they make an investment in the capacity of the teacher in front of them. But the investment does not end there. Additionally, every student who learns from the teacher is affected for the better. Each of these students immediately receives a stronger and more robust educational experience that strengthens their skill set and knowledge base that they carry forward to subsequent classes and future years. This investment continues to pay off beyond the given moment and impacts the future as well. Year after year, each student who passes through the doors of the classroom feels the effect of the improved abilities of the teacher.

Weak practices fall out of favor, and strong, compelling tactics become part of the daily routine. When a teacher embraces changes and the new actions and behaviors associated with it, a *new normal* is established. This new normal is the product of a quiet revolution that transforms the entire institution. Often, the old ways are swept away in such a subtle fashion that the old practices that were both accepted and defended disappear without a whimper.

The cumulative effect of efforts to improve instruction is not limited to the initial teacher who adopts the better practices. When one teacher gets better, it also has an influence on those teachers nearby. Collaborative team conversations take on a new significance and the result is felt at the grade or content level. Behind the individual discipline, the increased expectation begins to be felt throughout the school. The high tide lifts all boats. Without a formal announcement or proclamation, the new normal descends upon the entire school environment. The basic instructional expectation that becomes part of the fabric and culture of a school resets to a new normal.

This happens in very subtle and quiet ways. Teacher by teacher, conversation by conversation, as instructional practices are shored up, the whole of the school is transformed. Principals must use an optimistic view to fuel their efforts to drive instructional improvement toward positive change. Rather than focusing on the negative, the principal searches for the negative merely as an indicator for where next steps need to be taken. Once the needed change is identified, the focus moves away from the negative to the productive and positive possibilities that are preferable and expected.

Principals should remain sensitive to the reality of what their presence in the classroom signals. If each teacher observation is followed by an intense conversation focused on areas of improvement, teachers will soon be conditioned to fear and resent the principal's presence. This is unfortunate as it often occurs even with well-intentioned principals who are trying to be positive and helpful. Principals must recognize that timing is everything when discussing sensitive issues. Is there sufficient time to have the conversation that the principal truly needs to have? Has the principal noted a sufficient pattern in the behavior that would suggest a trend is developing?

Leaders must view relationships with their teachers like a bank account where they invest heavily in making deposits through healthy conversations before intending to make a significant withdrawal by discussing an instructional shortcoming. Otherwise, the presence of the principal in the classroom will be nothing more than a signal of upcoming professional anxiety. Principals must maintain enough of a presence in the classroom that neither the teacher nor the students are terribly surprised at the visit. They must also develop a trusting relationship so that the teacher does not come to expect a negative conversation after every classroom visit.

Indeed, the principal must embrace the understanding that for every teacher who struggles with one aspect of teaching, there are likely many others who excel in that particular area. In fact, principals should make a habit of noting any problems they are witnessing in the school setting and seek to find others immediately who do not struggle in that way. Before engaging a teacher who is exhibiting weak practices, the principal should spend some time in a classroom where a teacher engages in strong practices.

This can help a principal gain specific and concrete understanding of what doing the task well actually looks like. Indeed, some teachers may claim that it is not possible to do better than they are currently doing and having some firsthand examples to the contrary can be helpful. Obviously, it would not be prudent to throw a peer's performance in the face of a resistant teacher, but it is helpful to the principal to have evidence that their expectation is actually quite reasonable and possible.

Principals must seek out these "bright spots" in the school. Engaging a teacher in instructional dialogue because something they are doing is going better than anyone might expect is reaffirming to the teacher working hard to use best practices. In the following scenario, a principal continues to note that the level of questioning within social studies classrooms appears to be quite weak. The pattern seems to exist beyond one or two teachers. The administrator is unsure how to proceed without seeing what quality questioning technique actually looks like. She remembers that she once observed Ms. Riley engaging with her students in a lively debate, so she decides to observe her to see if the same troubling pattern extends to her classroom as well. The following is their conversation after school.

Principal: "I sure enjoyed visiting your class today. In particular, I was very intrigued by the questioning technique you were using with your students. Do you have a few minutes to help me understand your methods better?"

Teacher: "Sure! That's very nice of you to say."

Principal: "It seemed like you were asking a wide variety of types of questions that challenged your students in a healthy way. Do you have a system to make that happen?"

Teacher: "Well, I don't know that I'd call it an actual system, but I certainly do have a method to develop the questions I want to ask my kids."

Principal: "I am very interested in that. Can you help me understand it?"

Teacher: "Sure. It's not complicated, but it is very organized. First, I look at the state standard and note the verbs that the standard uses. There's a big difference in cognitive complexity between describing, explaining, and defending an argument, for example."

Principal: "Ok, that makes sense. So you have a target for what kids must do, right?"

Teacher: "Well, the substance of the question is really the target, but the verb tells me at what level the students must perform that task."

Principal: "Well, that does make good sense. But how did you operationalize that into the spectrum of questions I saw you asking today?"

Teacher: "Great question. So, I treat the cognitive level of the standard as the finish line. Then, I pull out a good old-fashioned cheat sheet of Bloom's Taxonomy. I think of all of the content I want my kids to know and I systematically work my way up the chart. I begin with low-level recall to help everyone get their bearings and then I march up the levels of complexity until I arrive at the expectation of the standard."

Principal: "Wow that sounds like a lot of preparation and work."

Teacher: "Not really. I first start by writing out every question I would like to ask. Then, I go back and erase the verbs from each question and systematically insert increasing levels of complexity. Just takes a few minutes really."

Principal: "I was very impressed with how engaged the students were and the quality of their answers."

Teacher: "That's not really very surprising at all. How can students give quality answers if they aren't asked quality questions?"

This principal has struck instructional gold. Teachers throughout the department are struggling with the very practice that Ms. Riley has mastered. The principal was able to accomplish a number of things with this interaction. Primarily, the leader learned that this problem, as pervasive as it may be, is not impossible to tackle. No one could now suggest that current inferior questioning practices are sufficient and that a better approach could not be expected.

The principal also exceled at noting the area of interest to discuss with the teacher but then allowed the teacher to voice the thinking behind the strong practice. The principal was not the expert in this conversation. There is no doubt that the teacher was flattered by both the recognition of the great practice and being able to help the principal better understand the work and skill that goes into being an excellent teacher.

The principal certainly made deposits into the relationship bank account. Further, the principal reinforced to this teacher that her work matters and that the principal also values good instruction. Above all, the principal learned important instructional technique in this exchange. Moving forward, every observation and conversation will be impacted by this unique approach this teacher is taking. Undoubtedly, the principal will soon find an opportunity to share this practice with the others in her department who are struggling and will benefit greatly from the example.

Principals need to be expert planners and organizers in many ways. One overlooked area that principals need to consider is the building-wide expertise in different instructional areas. If a principal keeps a thorough financial budget to ensure that there are sufficient funds to meet all of the building needs, it makes even more sense to design an organizational system to categorize expertise among all staff members. This may seem to be a strange task for a principal to pursue at first. However, principals keep a mental list about staff for less than noble reasons. Every principal could easily recite the names of staff members who fit in categories such as smart, lazy, superstars, hardworking, and pot stirrers. In fact, principals may have their top-five teachers they hope will never leave and those they would not choose to rehire if given the chance.

These mental lists are unfortunate because they tend to set up an opposition between the good guys and the bad guys as perceived by the principal. Further, these types of mental lists tend to overgeneralize and are not usually based on recorded, quantified data. Is the lazy teacher always lazy? Are there settings where this isn't true? Perhaps the principal has concluded that the teacher is lazy because he skipped lunch duty a few times. However, how would the principal reconcile the fact that this "lazy" teacher commits an extra ten hours a week to the local Rotary Club?

The reality is that everyone is far more complex than the mental categories where they are pigeon-holed. These generalizations serve no actionable purpose and limit a principal's ability to recognize and develop talents within the building. Principals should dump their mental lists and create actual spreadsheets to track the instructional capacity of staff. These topics need to move far beyond vague labels and represent the most important aspects of teaching.

For example, useful groupings would include teachers who excel in areas such as lesson planning, content knowledge, developing learning objectives, assessing student learning, and communicating with students. Obviously, there are far more categories that may be of interest for a principal to track. Looking at the categories that are valued on the school's adopted teacher evaluation instrument is a very wise place to begin. If the categories on that instrument describe excellent teaching, who possesses a particularly strong skill set in each of these areas?

One can easily imagine how powerful this exercise may prove to be. Principals might find that there are a few areas where everyone excels. Is this because it is valued in the school and has been the focus of professional development for the past several years? Perhaps the area that has received considerable attention does not have many high performers. Principals must decide what to make of that realization. Principals may find that there are certain critical instructional areas where no staff members are perceived to be strong. If the principal acknowledges it as an aspect of instruction that is important, what will the next steps be to build capacity in that area?

Unfortunately, principals may find that they are having a difficult time finding any area where a teacher excels. This is a critical moment for a principal as an instructional leader. If this is true, leaders must accept the fact that they cannot find a redeeming instructional quality in the teacher, but yet they are entrusting many students to that teacher's care on a daily basis. This is completely unacceptable. Principals must take immediate action to assist the teacher in her practice. Likewise, the principal must look inward and assess whether the previous conversations and evaluations with this teacher were conducted in an honest manner.

This is not the time to despair; rather, it is a time to embrace new work. In these moments, principals must spend the time to conduct a deep and thorough analysis of their struggling team member. It may be true that the teacher is not excelling in any category that it is noteworthy enough to be celebrated. However, principals must lead her to a new place. The best way to begin this work is to look for the brightest glimmer of potential in that teacher. The leader must look for personality traits that would lend them to growing in this area. Perhaps the teacher is highly organized. This is a trait that lends itself to excelling in instructional planning and preparation. The teacher may not yet apply those strong organizational skills to the classroom, but the potential is there.

Leaders must create the bridge between a natural quality of the teacher and how it can be best applied to the benefit of kids. Perhaps a teacher lacks organizational skills but has a warm and personable affect. With the help of the principal's guidance, this teacher may be able to use his relationship skills to lead others in developing interventions for struggling learners.

Leaders possess the distanced vantage point to see where raw personality traits can be molded into strong instructional traits. For many teachers, this happens quite naturally. For those who struggle, the leader may have to be the one who helps make the connection. Principals must be cautious that they begin the work capitalizing on the innate qualities of the person. Before asking a leopard to change its spots, it is far easier and sensible to use the raw materials that are already present.

A principal can be likened to a new parent in this regard. Often, parents begin to notice differences among their children and make judgments about the qualities that are displayed. For example, a parent may get frustrated that their younger child is not as compliant and obedient as their older sibling. The young sibling is assertive and needy and often is the one who is more likely to come into the house with scraped knees. In these moments, parents must take a deep breath and reflect that the calm demeanor of the older sibling may seem like a preferable quality, but maybe it is just a quality that makes for easier parenting. There will come a day where the quiet child needs to find a voice and assert himself and may lack the skills to do so because the parent appreciated his timid nature.

Likewise, the parent may tire quickly of patrolling the house to ensure the younger child doesn't get hurt due to their aggressive explorations of the countertops. But the bold and assertive nature of the younger child can prove to be a valuable quality on the day they need to stand up for what is right. Most qualities are neither good nor bad in themselves. They make people unique and poise them to excel in different ways. Teachers are no different. They bring forward natural qualities that allow them to excel in certain areas and also may lack other qualities that make them reticent to function in the way they are needed as educators.

Principals must commit to finding a strong suit for every teacher in their building. If a principal cannot find a potential area where a teacher may excel, that is ultimately an indictment against the leader rather than the teacher. Except in rare circumstances, leaders will be able to find promising qualities in all faculty members. For these individuals, principals are compelled to have serious conversations about whether they need to choose a new vocation. But for the rest, principals must commit to speculating what each teacher may look like at their very best.

Everyone is a work in progress possessing great potential. Much like an artist who is molding clay, principals need to consider what a teacher may look like when maximizing their potential rather than being mired in the pessimism of how they function without assistance and guidance. Owning this challenge is the very reason why a principal is needed. If teachers were not compelled to grow and get better, a principal may not even be needed in a school. Principals must embrace this chance to help others find a better way.

This exercise not only captures the potential of individuals, but it also begins to shape the landscape of where a school excels and where they need to focus more attention. Additionally, the principal has a firmer understanding of which teachers are most likely able to assist others in each of these areas. This type of planning and preparation allows the principal to move beyond the task of helping individual teachers with specific behaviors and positions the principal to begin making sweeping changes that transcend the entire school environment.

Once a principal has firmly established at least one potentially strong instructional trait in all staff members, the work then becomes an effort to expand the possibilities for each person. Finding one quality in each is necessary, but it is not sufficient. Principals cannot afford for this effort to be internalized by teachers as declaring the one, and only one thing that they do well. It is easy to imagine that some struggling teachers may take great solace in their newly discovered talent and over rely on that one trait. A teacher may conclude, "I may not assess student learning very well, but at least I have great relationships will kids."

This stance twists the very work the principal is trying to accomplish giving teachers an excuse to underperform is certain areas. Principals must remain vigilant in building upon whatever skills each person possesses. For some, this will take concerted efforts on a daily basis to keep certain teachers from back sliding in the quality of their instruction. For others, principals may only need to offer gentle guidance and suggestions to keep them stretching themselves as professionals.

Leaders must also guard against the tendency to become overly enamored with their most talented teachers. Principals can become star struck when observing their peers who excel in the classroom. In fact, principals can easily become intimidated if they recognize that the teacher's skill far surpasses their own knowledge and talents in the classroom. Administrators must accept the fact that they are called to lead those with the most talent as well. If this were not the case, no one would dare coach a professional sports team for fear of admitting that the coach was not better than the players on the team. Of course, this is ridiculous. In fact, many of the best coaches in history have had very mediocre skills themselves but have a talent for pushing and pulling the best from their players. This must be true for principals as coaches as well.

To extend the metaphor, the principal must take great care that the team is not overly reliant upon the superstars either. Strong teams are made up of many individuals each playing their part. Each team member must work to develop their own skills for the sake of the team and for the common good. Countless examples abound of superstar athletes who were never able to win at high levels because of their inability (or unwillingness) to build a strong team. These athletes have undeniably strong career statistics, but their inability to win at the highest levels must be noted. The whole point of team competition is to win. Fans often get overly excited about strong individual performances, but what does it really matter in the end if the team is unsuccessful?

Schools are made up of teams as well. As they say, it takes a village. Superstars in the classrooms indeed demonstrate all that is possible with a certain group of students, but all students deserve a superior experience and the superstar simply cannot teach them all. Principals must strive to increase the capacity of all teachers. The point is not to bring the all-star down to the level of others but to raise others to the highest of levels.

Principals must work to bring teachers together in this work. If teachers are left to work in isolation, they will not benefit from learning from each other.

This does not capitalize on shared efforts for improvement. However, working in isolation often spawns an even worse climate. When teachers begin hearing more about the work of others in their school from which they are disconnected, they are often given the impression that the school condones a state of "haves and have-nots." Teachers will undoubtedly tune in closely to determine if some teachers are benefiting from more time or resources in the instructional conversation than they are. This can be a precarious balance for a principal.

In response, principals must make a decision. It would be a mistake to respond to everyone in the same way. Principals should not give teachers the same amount of time and attention. Teachers do not necessarily expect that they receive the same thing from their principal. Principals, however, must ensure that they do give each teacher exactly what they need in the moment. This is no different from the way teachers respond to students. Each learner does not get exactly the same number of minutes from the teacher, but, rather, they get however much of the teacher's time and attention they require depending on their current need. If teachers perceive that the principal is attentive to their needs, it will stave off any theories that the principal values some at the expense of others.

Principals must recognize that their conversations and observations with teachers are one way they must build teacher's skills and capacity, but it is not the only way. Principals must be vigilant in finding opportunities to connect teachers with each other to build skills among the faculty. In the beginning, this must be done carefully as some teachers may not be willing to share and others may not be receptive to the advice. However, this is too powerful of an opportunity to fail to seize. In the following scenario, the principal finds an opportunity to make a connection between teachers.

Principal: "I wondered if you had a minute to chat about your lesson today."

Teacher: "Sure. Is there a problem?"

Principal: "Quite the opposite actually. I noticed you were doing something I've never seen before when your students were working through their writing prompt and wondered if you could help me understand it a bit better?"

Teacher: "The work we were doing writing summaries of nonfiction?"

Principal: "Yes, exactly. It appeared that you had a guide for them to follow in writing it."

Teacher: "Oh, that. Yes, talk about something learned from trial and error. I was getting so frustrated when I'd ask students to write a summary of a passage. They were terrible."

Principal: "What's your theory on that?"

Teacher: "It hit me like a ton of bricks. I was asking them to summarize a passage, but I had never taught them *how* to summarize. It sounds simple but it isn't. Let me ask you, explain how to summarize something without using the word *summary*."

Principal: "Wow. I never thought of it that way. It seems like an easy task, but I guess I'm struggling to explain what I'd say to a student."

Teacher: "Exactly. I have committed that I will never ask my students to do something I have not first taught them. I'd never taught them how to summarize, so I figured I needed to start there."

Principal: "How did they do?"

Teacher: "Much better. There is a technique to everything. Whether it is saddling a horse, playing the piano, or writing a summary, there is a technique that is required to do it well."

Principal: "What is the technique to writing a summary?"

Teacher: "Well, in my opinion, there are several steps in writing a summary. A student needs to skim the text to get a general idea of the topic, read the passage, find the main idea in the text, highlight important vocabulary, disregard unnecessary details, combine redundant examples, write a topic sentence from the main idea, and provide generalized supporting evidence."

Principal: "Yeah, I guess I would agree. I'm sure I wouldn't have come up with it on my own though!"

Teacher: "If that is true for you, imagine how a student would feel who is struggling to write well. This structure doesn't give them the answer, but it sure scaffolds their thinking in a way that allows them to get their own thoughts on paper."

Principal: "I must tell you how impressed I am with this. I was just talking to Mr. Chavira about a similar frustration he was having. Would you be willing to let me have a copy of the document you shared with the kids?"

Teacher: "Sure, I guess. If you think it would help."

Principal: "I really do. Are you okay if I send him your way if he wants to talk more about it?"

Teacher: "Yeah, I'd be glad to help."

From the beginning, the principal recognized the value in the work this teacher was doing. The principal had the humility to accept the role of learner as the teacher was allowed to be the expert in explaining the process and rationale. The principal learned many new things and was not too proud to pretend otherwise.

However, the principal did not allow the conversation to end there. The leader called to mind another teacher who was struggling in this way and sought to build a bridge between the two teachers. The principal was not overly aggressive by suggesting the teacher lead a faculty meeting on the subject. This teacher may not yet be completely comfortable with leading her peers. But, the principal recognized that she would be willing to engage in a quiet conversation with another teacher who sought her out. This is likely the beginning of a much bigger role for this teacher in the future. For now, though, easing her into a teacher leader role is most appropriate.

Proper caution is essential regarding the way in which a principal begins to make connections between staff members. Some conversations will be more natural and will allow the principal to proceed with an ease in facilitation compared to others. Principals should avoid trying to build these initial connections with either the most successful or the most struggling staff members. There will come a time to focus upon these groups, but they have unique characteristics that can be challenging to bridge. Teachers who struggle the most may be very hesitant to open up their practice to a peer. In fact, these teachers may be reluctant to reflect upon their struggles with their principal who has a supervisory obligation to address them. They will often shy away from observing others who are successful in the very ways in which they struggle.

Similarly, the most successful instructional practitioners may not be the best source to build initial connections. Their instructional approach is often far superior of others and can be off-putting to teachers who struggle. That is not to say that these excellent educators are not sensitive to other teachers. Often, they are very willing to help. However, if struggling teachers cannot begin to see themselves in the actions of a peer, bridging the gap in their performance seems unrealistic and disheartening. For the exemplary teacher, the light of their instructional excellence may serve to blind, rather than illuminate, their novice peers.

Principals can implement a couple of tactics to begin making connections between educators. Like the teacher in the aforementioned example, principals should look for teachers who have not turned their attention to helping their peers. Often, these teachers are willing to discuss their practices with others if they are coached and prompted a bit. Because they have not yet considered themselves to be the expert in professional circles, their mild approach is often more welcoming to struggling teachers. Those with weaker instructional practices often are able to keep their focus on the discussion of a new practice rather than being blinded by the talents of a celebrated teacher.

These newcomers to peer coaching initially do not see themselves as influencers of their peers. As good as they are in the classroom, working with other adults is not always part of their comfort zone. In fact, they often have not considered working much with their peers. These teachers often have a laser-like focus on teaching children and need to be coaxed into conversations with other adults. However, principals must search for teachers like these and urge them to consider expanding their professional engagement to the service of other teachers.

Because these teachers are typically intensely focused on students, it is often helpful to remind them that, by helping other teachers, they can actually assist a group of students beyond those on their roster. Principals can begin by surveying the landscape and identifying teachers with strong and confident instructional skills. Principals, for their part, need to approach these excellent teachers with a specific and appropriate struggling teacher in mind with whom they could begin to collaborate. Leaders must go slow in these first attempts to connect teachers. The purpose of the work is to connect people together, teacher by teacher. Individuals must find their way in this work before groups can be expected to do it. The underlying efforts by the principal are to build a strong foundation where the culture connects people with a common cause to help each other. Many hands make light work.

Principals should not limit the work of identifying potential influencers on their staff to a select few. They should also review their spreadsheet categorizing teachers by area of expertise and identify teachers who possess social capital among the staff. Natural dynamics emerge within a staff over time that results in certain people holding esteem with specific staff members. Perhaps two teachers were themselves childhood friends, or maybe they worked on college classes together. Many personal and professional ties bind staff members together in ways that are strong and deep. Most principals can readily identify these influential relationships in their staff, but most choose not to act upon those connections in a meaningful way.

Quite simply, principals may not possess enough personal influence to move a staff member as they wish and need to rely on others to convince that staff member to consider new work. Further, a staff member may not have established a respectful relationship with each and every teacher in their building. Many teachers work in the same building but do not know their neighboring teacher very well. As such, a principal may struggle to connect teachers simply because they do not know each other enough to begin professional conversations. Those with social capital can quickly build this bridge.

Although it may seem sadly ironic, the teacher who most needs assistance may not respond to the best instructor in the building, but they may respond to another teacher because they have coached together for the past ten years. Principals need to strategically recruit those with social capital to provide credibility to the improvement efforts. If a principal were to identify those most needing help, each of these teachers probably listens very closely to the advice of a peer. Principals must invest heavily in these social catalysts for assistance.

Principals must take active measures to keep strong instructional conversations growing within the school. These conversations may be competing with other topics that are far less important, but they are also in competition with strong voices on the staff that may have influence for all the wrong reasons. This can be easily witnessed in most faculty meetings that are not run with a focused agenda. In these meetings, certain voices quickly emerge and dominate the majority of the conversation.

Who are these people and in which direction do they attempt to drive the agenda? If it is in a positive direction, the principal may have an easy time in pushing an instructional agenda. However, most of these meetings turn in less than noble directions much to the irritation of the principal and the dismay of focused teachers. Principals should note the teachers whose thoughts and opinions they value the most and recognize how seldom they may find their voice in those meetings. If a meeting allows wise voices to be silenced and empowers only the loudest among the group, the principal is wasting precious collaboration time.

Some teachers are simply more extroverted and vocal than others. This is not necessarily good or bad. It is, however, important to note that they may dominate the conversation. Whose voice are they drowning out and what might that person have to say? Principals must reflect whether they create any environments or forums where shy voices lacking confidence among their peers have a chance to weigh in on important matters.

Principals must also pay close attention to the weight that seniority plays within their school. Of course, this is not to suggest that those with experience do not have wisdom to impart. However, every principal recognizes that, while many of the best teachers are veterans of the profession, many very weak teachers also have many years on the job. Unfortunately, seniority has become a lazy way to decide important matters within a building. Principals must rethink whether seniority determines decisions such as class load or teaching assignments. Allowing senior members of a staff to dictate which levels and courses they will teach is to abdicate one of the most important aspects of principal leadership.

The principal is the only professional in the building with intimate details of each teacher's expertise and struggle. The stakes are too high for kids to leave these decisions to the whims of whichever teacher has an earlier hire date. For example, principals may have teachers within their science department vying for the chance to teach an advanced placement course in a high school. Should the person who has taught longer in the building automatically be awarded the assignment? Principals must reflect deeply on how much that trait is valued compared to other qualities such as educational background in that content area, other professional experiences, and a track record of student achievement. Oftentimes, the most senior staff member will also possess many of these other prized qualities. Seniority should be a characteristic that allows for other important instructional qualities to have been developed. It should not be the sole reason a voice is valued.

A similar obstacle inhibiting progressive voices from emerging in the school is the argument that the school should not change because, "This is how we do it here." Overcoming the inertia of past practices can be a daunting task for any principal. Every environment has systems in place to accomplish the tasks that the employees view as necessary. However, there are often few checks and balances in these systems to gauge if the current approach actually focuses on the most important things in education.

Beyond that, it is unclear whether the school is achieving at high levels with their historic approach. A school's current approach produces a certain level of achievement. If the school were to do things exactly the same, it would likely continue producing the similar results. If, however, a principal desires that the students achieve at higher levels, teachers must either quit engaging in certain behaviors or begin engaging in other ones. In a system that values the way things have always been done, traditional voices tend to be the only ones that are valued.

The only time other voices may find traction is when a fresher face echoes the same sentiment that is traditionally espoused in the school. Principals must take active steps to articulate very clearly what the current levels of performance are and in what ways it falls short of the ideal. Noting the gap between where the school is and where the principal wants it to be is the key to moving beyond the state where traditional voices are the only ones that are valued.

Sometimes the voices that are valued in a building are more formal and find their footing within the context of a predefined group or committee. Schools often develop standing committees such as a building leadership team and a school improvement steering committee to guide improvement efforts in the school. Principals must recognize that these groups may be engaged in consequential work, but this is not always the case. The principal should revisit the reason for the committee's existence and review past agendas to see if they are focused on appropriate work.

For example, if a school improvement committee is focused on revamping the school's tardy policy, it has veered away from the heart of the most important instructional work that should be addressed. Principals certainly need to attend to tardy students, but capturing a group under the guise of school improvement and focusing on small attendance infractions is simply a waste of time and opportunity. Principals must take an active role in keeping the proper focus of these groups and committees.

Aside from maintaining an appropriate instructional focus for these groups, a principal must also review who is on the committees. If principals want to ensure representation from a wide variety of stakeholders, they must question if some voices have been left out of the conversation. These formal committees are often tasked with important matters, and they give the appearance of a comprehensive approach to addressing complicated topics. If the committee makeup is artificially contrived, it can limit the ability for voices to be heard within the very structures that were created to ensure a wide range of voices. Principals should reflect whether membership to all committees ought to be opened up to all faculty. While some will undoubtedly choose not to attend, it assures that the message is not sent that some people are not welcome to contribute.

Leaders should actively inquire among the faculty, "Whose voice is not being heard on this subject?" Taking feedback on this question assures that there are not missing voices in the conversation and sends a very strong public statement that all voices are valued. When the principal feels comfortable that all voices are able to contribute to important issues, it is then important to take active steps to nurture and protect the voices in the minority on the issue. Figuring out which opinion has been marginalized and for what reason is critical to keep the dialogue from becoming one-dimensional. Principals must reaffirm the sentiment that good ideas will stand on their own merit and bad ideas will wither on the vine. Bad ideas do not need to be silenced. On the contrary, all ideas must be heard regardless of who is holding the opinion. In the end, the best ideas will be embraced for the right reasons.

Taking this approach sends a strong message that everyone can have a voice in the most important matters within the school environment. This radically redefines who is able to work intimately on topics of great instructional consequence, and teachers are not limited in the role they can choose to play. When teachers begin to believe that there has not been a preordained group of *deciders* on staff, everyone is emboldened and empowered to help. This immediately dismantles anyone's theories that some teachers are the favorites of administration.

Principals must guard against these inaccurate suppositions. Of course, these theories are easy to embrace because a principal is not likely to divide time equally between every staff member. Some staff spend more time with a principal than others. On occasion, this is because the teacher has greater needs and demands it from the principal. Likewise, a principal may either consciously or unconsciously begin to spend more time and engage in more conversations with some teachers rather than others. Leaders must reflect deeply on this reality and ask themselves who currently gains the benefit of their time and attention.

More importantly, for what reasons do some staff garner the most attention? Principals must be honest in their appraisal of these matters. Teachers will notice if the principal chooses to engage with some of their peers on social topics rather than work-related issues. If a teacher does not feel welcomed in friendly conversations, they will certainly be reluctant to discuss matters of greater importance. The best way to do this is to acknowledge that any teacher can command significant portions of the principal's time if they are focused on the most important instructional issues for students and is committed to the improvement of practices at both a personal and system-wide level.

Chapter 6

Leading the Reluctant

At the heart of all change efforts is the hope that groups of people come together and begin to do their work better by doing things differently. In any social environment, there are countless opinions of what should be changed and how things should be done. Likely, reasonable people will recognize that some ideas are good, some are bad, and with some ideas, it is too early to tell. Most people show a bit of reluctance when first hearing a new idea. This is actually quite healthy. Approaching any new idea with caution is prudent to ensure that ideas are not entertained that would, in effect, put things in a worse condition than the current state of affairs.

A healthy bit of skepticism not only protects against adopting bad ideas, but it also guards against the tendency for people within systems to make changes constantly depending upon the prevailing winds. Beginning with a desire to understand a new idea more thoroughly before automatically supporting it is a great starting point. However, many people struggle to move from their current belief system and consider the prospect of adopting new practices. Every educator has undoubtedly heard peers respond negatively to a newly proposed idea. Imagine that an excited teacher ventures into a discussion with peers about a new idea the principal proposed in a staff meeting. Likely, the teacher will hear comments such as:

"We've tried that before, but it didn't work."
"There are too many things on our plate already. When are they going to take something off?"
"This too shall pass."
"If we don't do anything, he will forget about it soon enough."
"Looks like our principal must have gone to a conference recently and has come back with another big idea that won't work with our kids."

Responses such as these can easy dishearten those who are intrigued by a new idea. Certainly, the principal has a monumental task ahead to bring these reluctant teachers along in their thinking. Might there be a bit of truth in any one of these statements? Certainly, they may represent how other ideas have come and gone in their school over the years. Keep in mind, those other ideas were probably a combination of both good and bad ideas. If a bad idea was adopted previously and it is resurfacing, it may be very appropriate to conclude, "We've tried that before and it didn't work."

The true problem with statements like these is that they seem to be an attempt to end a conversation rather than enrich it. If stating that the idea had been tried before and did not work was coupled with a sincere question about how it might be reconsidered differently this time, the conversation remains healthy and productive. Indeed, it may refine the proposal into a better version than ever before considered. Likewise, if a teacher were to suggest that "if we don't do anything, he will forget about it soon enough," this may be an insight into the way in which change efforts have been treated historically. Perhaps this comment was made out of frustration that good ideas always seem to have shallow roots that soon blow away in the winds of newer change.

Again, these responses should be seen as the beginning of a conversation rather than the end of one. Principals should seize these seemingly negative responses and find the kernel of truth within them. Regardless, if a principal seeks to transform those negative responses, the newly proposed idea better be marketed in such a fashion that even a naysayer is left with the conclusion that this idea seems fundamentally different and better than other proposals in the past.

It is the work of the leader to support only the best of ideas and to lead the staff through the change process. If teachers are reluctant to adopt a new idea, it often has to do with the way in which it was sold. Leaders may have a deep understanding of what they want to do and why, but packaging that into a healthy sort of argument that is convincing to stakeholders is another matter entirely. A leader must recruit believers into a new way of thinking. Certainly, there are some people who tend to be early adopters with any idea and throw themselves willingly into new work. Likewise, there are others whose default mode seems to be one that resists or even blocks any new ideas being presented.

If an idea is worth supporting, it is worth being messaged well. This messaging is completely within the control of the building leader. Principals often mistakenly begin talking about a proposal before taking the time to craft the message around the idea. This is a mistake. When teachers hear a new idea for the first time, a principal has a narrow window of opportunity to ensure that the message around the idea is thoughtful and sound.

In order to put together a compelling argument to recruit believers, the leader must understand that reluctant people tend to respond in one of three distinct ways. While any given person will not necessarily respond in one way consistently, a principal must consider that the message conveyed needs to account for all three possibilities in order to capture the spectrum of reasons why staff members become adopters of an idea. Moreover, a leader should be heartened to know that every staff member can be brought on board with one of these three approaches. By carefully constructing this messaging, a principal is assured that *all* teachers will implement the proposed idea.

People are moved out of their initial reluctance to adopt an idea by being converted, convinced, or contained. For any new idea a principal considers that requires buy-in from teachers, leaders must tailor a version of the message for these three possible responses. Some teachers will become believers because the principal *converts* their thinking through a heartfelt emotional response. Other teachers adopt an idea because a principal has *convinced* them through a logical set of reasons and arguments. The final group of teachers is not touched in either the heart or the head, and a leader must *contain* their behaviors around the proposed idea.

The greatest of things can happen when the hearts of good people are moved. When the hearts of people are touched, it resonates within their very moral center and inspires commitment and action. When people begin to associate the work at hand with who and what they are called to be as people, accepting a new set of practices is typically not much of a problem to be resolved.

Making a connection between the type of work that needs to be done by eliciting a powerful emotional response is imperative for the leader. If the proposed work is not of heartfelt consequence in the lives of kids, it may not be work that is really very important. Principals must reflect on the actions needed on the part of teachers and determine what the consequences will be for children if the work is not done. Leaders must seize upon these consequences and message them to staff in a way that intentionally engages a movement of their heart.

Principals must ensure the emotionally charged plea being made is, in fact, genuine. Because the leader is seeking to inspire others in a way that is touching, the message cannot be superficial or contrived. Trying to pass trite sentimentality off as an inspiring message of hope for children must be avoided. Not only will this fail to resonate with teachers seeking to connect their work with their heart, but it will be seen as a manipulative attempt to coerce others into action for all of the wrong reasons. This is often seen in education when someone attempts to push a particular agenda by adding the notion that the idea is "good for kids." A statement like this is typically nonsense. Using this expression in a vague sort of way gives the impression that others knowingly make decisions that are not good for kids. Sending this sort of message is entirely counterproductive. Principals must clearly define the problem, describe the proposed idea, and then paint a picture of the ways in which kids will benefit in new and important ways because of teachers adopting a new set of actions. Teachers want to be moved in this way.

All educators want to know that their work is of significance and consequence. Leaders must tap into this strong desire to make a difference and connect their work to that possibility. When this is done well, teachers will truly become converted. In fact, principals must be prepared that this can elicit strong emotional reactions in teachers. Leaders must be ready to assist teachers who exhibit a need for support if they are truly touched and inspired to act.

Being converted in one's thinking to accept that they are able to change the life of a young person in a profound way is a tremendous gift that comes with great responsibility. Some teachers may react to this prospect in a very emotional manner, and principals must be ready to encourage and support them through the acceptance of this role. Likewise, sometimes teachers react emotionally out of guilt for failing to intervene for kids up to this point. Principals must be prepared to focus the work on what teachers are obliged to do next rather than feel remorse for failing to act up to this point. In the following example, the principal has crafted a message intended to convert teachers to intervene for struggling readers in their high school.

Principal: "Ladies and gentlemen, across this nation, one out of every four adults lacks the ability to read at functional levels. In the most prosperous country in the history of our world, we offer children a free education for thirteen years and yet some do not leave us with the very gift that is the reason for our existence. We are educators. When we teach, kids learn. But even in our own school, we have many walking the halls that would not be able to read the very words written on the diploma they seek. I propose that we end this cycle of illiteracy once and for all. Can we draw a line in the sand at this moment and promise that no student will leave us in this condition?

I'd like to take a moment to introduce you to one of our students. Her name is Jenna. For those of you who do not know her, she is seventeen years old and is a senior in our school. Many of you are responsible in helping her along the way. It is not been easy for her. When she became pregnant past year, her parents kicked her out of the house and she now is raising her baby and living with her older sister in an apartment. Although Jenna has not dropped out, she is a struggling reader. Maybe you have seen her baby at one of our basketball games. Every time I look at her little boy, it bothers me deeply that Jenna may not be able to read the labels on the medicine bottles when he gets sick. I know our social worker helped her install the car seat properly because she could not read the directions and follow them. I wonder how many other ways her little one is at a disadvantage because she is not able to read very well.

We have one more year left with Jenna before she leaves us. I am asking if we can make a promise to her little boy that we will not let Jenna leave our school without becoming a stronger and more functional reader. This will not be easy, but it is critically important. Of course, I would not feel confident in asking just anybody if they are up to this task. But you all are different. In this school, when we say we care about everyone, we mean everyone. Jenna needs our help. Can we all commit to increasing our own skills in helping our kids become better readers and give her the type of practice she is going to need to be able to function when she leaves our care?"

This impassioned plea by the principal does not unfairly emotionally hijack the teachers. Everything the principal has said is rooted in fact. There are students who leave public schools and cannot read their own diploma. It is sad, but it is also true. Further noting that Jenna may struggle with her literacy in a way that can compromise the safety of her child is irrefutable. Many well-educated people must take a double look at the directions in administering medicine for their child. The difficulty for someone who is subliterate is even more troubling. This principal does a fine job in reminding the staff that the work they are engaged in is very high stakes. However, the principal does not attempt to make the staff feel guilty about the events that have led up to this point. Just because Jenna's situation is their problem, it does not mean that it is their fault. The principal passionately argues that the staff, however, is her only solution.

The principal has led this staff to a decisive moment. While the principal cannot guarantee how each staff member will respond to the challenge that has been set before them, they are at a fork in the road in how they will decide. Moreover, each teacher will be forced to decide what to make of the principal's attempt at conversion. Will their hearts be moved sufficiently to act? It is unlikely that all teachers will be converted by the moral mandate that the principal has set before them. However, the ones that will convert will be strong allies for Jenna moving forward. They will have drawn a connection between their moral center and the work that is being asked of them. This will give their new work incredibly strong purpose, and it will intertwine the new work with their very vocation in life.

Some teachers will not always be moved to action by a principal's attempt at conversion. This is not to suggest that they lack empathy or that they are not emotionally invested in their work. In reality, everyone is moved to action by some things, but not others. Not every person contributes to every fundraising campaign that shows up on their doorstep. People are emotionally complex, and often the best efforts by the principal to draw that connection between their work and their heart are not enough to bring people into new practices. For those who remain, principals should craft a new message. Instead of converting the heart, the principal needs to convince their minds. At times, people make decisions from their heads not their hearts. This is an incredibly persuasive way to motivate people as well.

Principals should craft a message that appeals to logic and common sense. Unfortunately, many of the professional obligations teachers have are not always sensible. Teachers are obliged to do things, but are uncertain why it is required. Perhaps some teachers continue to engage in these actions out of habit, but likely most teachers will resist new work especially if it is physically and mentally demanding, and they cannot understand the thinking behind it. Leaders should clearly define the need, explain the proposed solution, and then bridge the two by discussing how it is the most sensible way to proceed.

Providing a sound rationale for a new idea is all that it takes for some people to embrace their work with vigor. This is especially true if the principal can highlight the reasons why the proposed work makes more sense than the current approach. Even reluctant teachers may be willing to swap out one way of doing things for another if the old way is shown to be outdated and unnecessary.

The principal in the aforementioned example crafted a strong message for emphasizing literacy in the high school attempting to convert teachers' hearts. Because some of the teachers were not sufficiently moved to change their practices, the principal continued with a message focused on trying to convince the remaining staff members:

Principal: "It certainly can be argued that students in poverty often struggle to grow adequately over time to function at grade level. Our state exam scores would show that indeed we have a lower percentage of poor students who are proficient in reading. But I must note that we have found success with 45 percent of our students in poverty, right? Being poor has not been automatically synonymous with illiteracy."

It is true that Jenna is a teen mom. She has a lot on her plate and is not as able to focus time and energy on her studies like she was previously. But she certainly would not be the first teen mom to find success in our building. We have had many young ladies who were incredibly successful with us who had a baby at home. We have done it before. How can we replicate the success for Jenna?

I'd like to draw your attention to the screen at the front of the room. I have an excerpt from the U.S. government final exam projected on the screen. Jenna will need to be able to read this and understand it sufficiently to answer seven questions on the final. Of course, U.S. government is a required course for graduation. What if Jenna understands the concepts in U.S. government but fails the course because she cannot read the passage? Is this test actually a reading test for her? I have now also put up an excerpt from a novel she is reading in her intervention class. The book is challenging her and is calculated at a fifth-grade reading level. Jenna has been with us for four years now. What we have done up to this point has not worked. Our efforts have not sufficiently closed the gap. I would argue that we need to begin doing something different.

I have one last slide I would like to show you. I have compared our state exam results to all of the other schools in the state. I have removed schools larger than us and those that are smaller than us. I have removed those with both higher and lower numbers of special education students and those with differing poverty levels. I have also limited the comparison to those who have similar demographics in race and ethnicity. We are left with twelve schools in the state that are incredibly comparable to us. On the basis of percentage of students who are proficient in reading on the state exam, what place do you think we rank? As it turns out, we are eighth out of the twelve. I do not believe we should be satisfied with that. Others who look just like us are doing better. Our district curriculum director has compiled a list of reading interventions that meet rigorous third-party review standards for quality. Our intervention committee has vetted them all and is recommending the one that was at the top of the list for showing the strongest results. Can we commit to adopting this new program to intervene for our students?"

The principal certainly shifted the tone away from an emotional appeal to a logical rationale for change. As a leader, the principal recognized that the task at hand was difficult. It is important not to diminish the complexity of the problem needing solved. Oversimplifying a complicated situation will immediately destroy the logical argument that is being constructed in the first place. However, the principal wisely notes that, as complicated as the situation may be, the staff has successfully navigated students like Jenna through these difficult waters. This is crucial. Every logical point has an underlying purpose of cinching up every loophole someone may offer as an excuse to justify a student failing within the system.

Noting the occasions where staff has been successful not only is a compliment to them for their efforts but also reminds them of their ability to wield control over difficult circumstances. This effectively silences anyone who might suggest it cannot be done. The principal does not have to refute that claim is based purely on hope. Rather, past practices prove it has been done. Likewise, showing the actual text that a student is able to read compared to the level of text she needs to read brings a theoretical argument of literacy gaps into a very concrete view. Teachers can glance back and forth between the obvious differences in vocabulary, sentence structure, and sophistication. Even those untrained as reading teachers will immediately note the difference. This difference is the gap that needs filled.

The principal's comments about Jenna struggling with content because of underlying reading issues forces teachers to reconcile a dissonance created when students may have mastered course material but struggle regardless. In this moment, teachers are forced to decide how to proceed when they think they are assessing course content but are, in fact, assessing something entirely different. This is not to suggest that rigorous reading ought to be stripped from content courses. In fact, quite the contrary. It actually demonstrates the way in which literacy is inextricably bound up in a student's ability to perform in content classes. Students must have skills in both. Hopefully, this can convince staff that improving disciplinary literacy skills will result in stronger students in their course content as well.

The principal ends the persuasive argument noting that Jenna has been in their care for a number of years and is not thriving with current efforts. Likewise, the problem extends beyond Jenna as the statewide results show the school underperforming even when isolating the comparison to similar schools. This argument has the effect of demonstrating a logical need to incorporate a school-wide effort rather than limiting the work to new interventions for Jenna. In this example, it is important to put a face on the problem, but the principal must also argue that she is merely emblematic of a much bigger problem. Once again, by offering examples of others who have produced a better result, the principal closes a loophole arguing that better results are simply not possible. On balance, the principal has constructed an argument that must be considered. If teachers remain reluctant to join in the work, it is not because the facts are refutable. The principal has designed the rationale in a way that is absolutely true. At this point, teachers must decide if it is convincing enough to act.

Of course, there often remains a group of teachers whose hearts and minds are unmoved despite the best attempts by a principal to inspire teachers to conversion and to convince them through a rational explanation. These remaining teachers cannot be ignored. Unfortunately, principals have often done just that and have ignored their unwillingness to join in required work. Realistically, these reluctant teachers have often been neglected by administrators after voicing their reluctance. These teachers will undoubtedly evolve from their reluctant position and will become resistant to the effort in time. A principal must take active measures to bring these people into the work as well. However, the way in which this is done is different from the previous two approaches.

Before proceeding any further, principals must make a commitment of their own. Leaders must decide if this proposed work is indeed going to be the expectation for teachers moving forward. There can be no middle ground where the principal would prefer if they cooperated but will be unresponsive otherwise. If principals cannot decide if an idea is required or if they decide the idea is optional, they must admit to their stakeholders that the idea will only be implemented in pockets and that some students may not reap the benefits of the new work. It should be noted that not every initiative needs to be required of all staff and students. Perhaps some efforts are beginning as a grassroots effort, and a principal desires to let it blossom on its own for a time without mandating required action by all. This approach is often appropriate.

However, principals must ask themselves the very pointed question whether each issue ought to be optional for some or required for all. For those issues that a principal decides must be adopted by all, the implementation must be seen in a new light. While the principal may try to convert and convince followers on both optional and requirement reform efforts, the final strategy of containment is reserved only for the staff who are not yet on board but the initiative is required.

If the prior efforts seek to convert their hearts and convince their heads, the final tactic must effectively contain their hands. This strategy is constructed to encourage and limit the range of acceptable behaviors that teachers can adopt around the new initiative. Before a principal creates that plan, it is imperative to realize that teachers will respond in a number of ways if their behaviors are not contained. Some may ignore the new work and proceed along professionally as if nothing new is happening around them. Others may resent the new work and begin to resist and block the work in more active ways. Not only do these responses put some students in a position where they do not get to benefit from the changes happening in their school, but these reluctant blockers can begin to unravel good work that is happening with others. If some teachers can be converted and convinced, it is also quite possible that they can backpedal in their commitment if a peer is whispering negativity into their ears. A principal cannot abide with a divided house on these kinds of matters and must intervene.

When principals make the decision to intervene, they must resist the urge to respond emotionally to the lack of commitment on the part of a teacher. Up to this point, the principal has only painted the emotional and intellectual picture of why the work should be done. The leader has not yet made clear what the expectation is for the teachers. Even the converted and convinced need to hear very specific examples of what must be done. This is especially true for those the principal must contain. If principals have committed to implementing this new work and have decided that participation is nonnegotiable, they must then clearly articulate the specific, expected behaviors that are required. Principals must decide what teachers must do, to what degree they must do them, and how often they are to be done. Further, the principal must clearly state the artifacts that will be produced to ensure that the work is being done with fidelity.

Principals should recognize that their expectations for staff do not exist in a vacuum but rather play out in a social context saturated by power struggles and politics. This is a time for a principal to link the present work with a well-established portion of the teacher's job description. Whether a disgruntled teacher calls a district administrator, a board member, or enlists the support of a teachers' union, a principal can often be forced to explain the rationale for a decision that seems to make good sense to everyone but those most able overrule the decision. Therefore, principals should make explicit reference to the portion of a district's mission, strategic plan, or improvement goals that most closely align to the proposed work. This creates a direct line between the work that everyone agrees should be done with the newly proposed idea.

When presenting the next steps in implementing the proposal, a principal can build off of a strong foundation by stating, "In keeping with section two of our district improvement plan to develop comprehensive academic interventions to those who are reading below grade level, we will now begin implementing the following three action steps in our school." Creating these links establishes clarity of purpose behind new requirements for teachers and should be widely acknowledged as the reasons why the work is essential.

Perhaps the strongest link that a principal can make between established professional obligations and new initiatives is through the teacher's evaluation instrument. This requires delicate and thoughtful messaging but can be an incredibly powerful lens to describe professional duties. Leaders must great care to use the evaluation instrument continually as a way to describe all aspects of a teacher's job description. This instrument should clearly articulate the wide variety of responsibilities a teacher has in great detail. For example, most evaluation models differentiate between components such as lesson planning, assessment, and communication with families. These aspects are all very distinct but are certainly part of the job expectation. Because teachers are formally evaluated on the model, they can easily begin to associate it with the tool that principals use to terminate employees. This is most unfortunate. Instead, principals must use the evaluation documents as a learning tool to describe in great detail what doing the job well encompasses.

Most evaluation instruments have greatly detailed rubrics that describe teachers who are unsatisfactory, basic, proficient, and distinguished in their practices. Principals should reference these documents frequently to describe how teachers' efforts are demonstrating their success as a teacher. If a teacher volunteers to be on the district calendar committee, principals should make reference to the way the teacher is now excelling in the portion of the instrument that requires teachers to contribute to the school and district. If principals make connections to the ways in which teachers are demonstrating success on the evaluation model, it becomes much easier to discuss occasions where their actions fall short of the requirements of the model.

Principals need to identify which section of the evaluation instrument supports the work that is now being required. If the principal is asking that teachers engage in more formative assessments of their students, that principal needs to reinforce that this work is the way in which they demonstrate their proficiency on the category for assessing student learning.

For the new initiative, the principal must list the discrete steps a teacher is required to take to meet expectations and the portion of the teacher performance model it helps to fulfill. Whether teachers have been converted, convinced, or must be contained, everyone must be very clear on what doing the work well demands. Up to this point in the scenario, the principal has done excellent work in trying to win the hearts and heads of the staff by creating a sound rationale for adopting new practices with struggling readers. However, the principal has not yet articulated what exactly must be done. Without taking this next step, reluctant teachers cannot yet be contained in their behavior and those who are willing may not know exactly what to do next. At this point, the principal may add:

> Because of the severe academic needs for many of our students, we will now begin implementing a series of steps to address the issue. Beginning Friday, our instructional coaches will begin providing professional development for every teacher on disciplinary literacy strategies during our designated times. We will introduce a new protocol each week and ask you to implement it in your classroom instruction. The subsequent week, I am asking you to bring back student work from the implemented protocol and we will spend ten minutes debriefing on its effectiveness.

The principal has not rolled out the entirety of the literacy plan at this point. That could prove to be information overload. However, teachers are clear that their next steps include attending a Friday staff development session, learning a new technique, implementing that technique during the next week, and bringing back student work to discuss progress. Every teacher now knows that these four steps are required practices. The converted and the convinced appreciate the clarity of direction and look forward to the work to address this academic deficiency being exhibited by students. Those who remain reluctant have a decision to make.

As the next week unfolds, it will be very easy for the principal to determine if the reluctant behaviors have disappeared. It is important to require a very quick turnaround for work to be produced in order that long periods of time do not elapse between mandating new work and being able to check in on the progress teachers are making. In the final segment of the reading intervention scenario, the principal engages in a conversation with Mr. Williams about his participation:

Principal: "Thanks for stopping by on your prep period. I'd like to visit with you about our recently adopted reading initiative."

Teacher: "Sure. I thought what you said in our meeting made a lot of sense."

Principal: "Well, help me understand what you have done thus far on your end."

Teacher: "I was at the staff development training past Friday. You can ask Mr. Long if you'd like. We sat together."

Principal: "Yes, I'm aware that you attended. I'm not sure if you saw me, but I stopped by and looked in for a minute. It appeared that you were grading papers during the instructional coach's mini-lesson."

Teacher: "I was listening. You know, I've had all of this stuff before. Just multitasking, I suppose."

Principal: "I am asking that you refrain from outside distractions during the training. If you'll recall our code of cooperation, we all jointly agreed that we will put away distractions during meeting times out of respect to others."

Teacher: "Ok, sure. Bad habit, I guess."

Principal: "Mr. Williams, I also did not receive a copy of the instructional protocol we all agreed to use this week highlighting student work on a reading prompt. Can you give me a copy now?"

Teacher: "I'm afraid not. I got swamped this week and wasn't able to get around to it."

Principal: "Mr. Williams, I made it clear in our faculty meeting that this work is not optional for any teacher. I will be having this conversation with everyone who did not give it an honest effort."

Teacher: "Can I be honest? This feels like one more thing on our plates. I'm very overwhelmed and stressed right now."

Principal: "Let's talk a bit more about that. I understand that you feel like there is a lot going on and there is. As educators, we must do many things simultaneously. But I must disagree that this is one more thing on your plate. Helping students find success who are struggling with basic skills is not something on your plate, it is the plate."

Teacher: "Yeah, I suppose. It's just frustrating. My training is as a business teacher. I don't even know how to teach kids to read. It really feels like I'm doing someone else's job. No one helps me teach business concepts, you know?"

Principal: "Mr. Williams, if students cannot functionally read, they will never find success in your business class or anywhere else. It is a fundamental. I would agree that your training up to now may not have included this sort of support for our students. But the job description has changed. Folks on the assembly line are not making cars the way their fathers did either. We must adapt to the need. This is our current need and it is my expectation for you."

Teacher: "Okay."

Principal: "We have designed our Friday trainings to give you the support you need. Is there anything else I can do to offer you assistance in meeting this expectation?"

Teacher: "No, I got it. I guess I just didn't completely get how important this is to you."

Principal: "It is important to me, Mr. Williams. I hope it becomes more important to you in time. Regardless, I want to do everything I can to ensure that students get this extra help and that you continue to meet your professional obligations. If I can summarize, you need to attend every Friday training and participate without distraction. You need to incorporate the protocol you learn in class with your students the following week, and you need to bring completed student work for discussion. I will ask that you bring the student work to me before school on Friday morning so we can visit together about it before taking it to your group. Do you have any other questions for me?"

Teacher: "Nope. Got it."

The principal began this conversation by making sure that there was sufficient time to discuss the issue. Before hearing otherwise, the principal could not be sure that this would be a brief meeting. Likewise, the principal peeled away the state of events slowly, acknowledging that the teacher had complied with one aspect of the requirement by attending the meeting. The principal saved some time in revealing the teacher's uncooperative behavior by witnessing it firsthand. In anticipation for a range of commitment to the new work, it was wise for the principal to observe the teachers rather than rely on secondhand reports from the frustrated instructional coach.

The principal clarified that merely attending is insufficient and that the teacher needed to participate fully in order to meet the expectation. The principal then asked for a copy of the student work. Of course, the teacher may have done it and the principal should not assume the worst. By asking for the student work, it brought the issue to a head immediately and steered the teacher away from the temptation to be deceptive about practices that had not occurred.

The teacher then tried to derail the conversation about meeting expectations by entering into a friendly debate about teacher workloads and preparation. The principal briefly engages that the expectations are indeed appropriate and reasonable. Without resorting to threats of insubordination, the principal very clearly indicates that the teacher needs to fulfill all professional expectations and that the principal is happy to provide additional support and assistance if necessary. This frames the conversation in a healthy way where the teacher's success in the classroom remains the desired outcome.

The principal ends the conversation by asking to see the work product the following week. This move sends a strong message that not only is it required to engage in meaningful work, but at least for the short term, the teacher's work will be viewed more closely by the principal until all of the required behaviors are completed. While both the teacher and the principal may prefer not to engage in these pointed conversations, the leader must recognize that they are essential and can be conducted without negative emotions coming to the surface.

As difficult as they may be, they are far easier than trying to pick up the pieces of a poorly implemented intervention within the school. Because the principal quickly attended to the reluctant teacher, it is unclear whether the teacher would have come around in time or if this was only the beginning of a more vocal and defiant rejection of the required work.

Principals and others in the educational conversation often cite the term "push back" to describe the reluctance of others to join in important work. Whenever this is invoked, a principal should probe much deeper into the reason why they believe there will be push back from others surrounding the work. This term seems to be invoked as a veiled threat of sorts. "You better be careful implementing these changes, there's going to be a lot of push back." A comment such as this should not be quickly dismissed.

Principals must ask follow-up questions to determine what is being implied in the comment. Typically, it is voiced in an effort to change the leader's mind about implementing new work. Rarely, it is used to indicate how the work could be modified to make it more streamlined and efficient. Principals should be skeptical of this response. It is often used as a way to put a respectable face on the desire for educators to keep harmony among the adults in the building at all costs. These educators would suggest that merely asking someone to engage in additional work, even if it is good for children, could present a strain on the relationships between the adults in the setting.

According to this logic, the very culture and climate of the school is dependent on what is required of them in completing their professional duties. Principals must reveal this absurd response for what it is. Certainly, leaders should not be engaging in unnecessary work in the first place, but some very demanding work is absolutely necessary. Doing what is right for students and maintaining harmony among the adults are not mutually exclusive. A principal must guard against those who would seek to define work in this manner.

When a principal is forced to contain the behaviors of teachers to ensure fidelity of the work, it is certainly not ideal. Preferably, all teachers will join together to implement important work, but this is rarely the case. Principals across the nation expend considerable energies in simply trying to get all staff to adopt agreed-upon best practices in instruction. While containing the behaviors of certain teachers is not the preferable or optimal approach, it does ensure that everyone is engaging in the same positive behaviors despite having different motivations.

It is important to note that many behaviors are improved if a person is converted or convinced of an idea, but it is not necessarily dependent on it. If a teacher is merely compliant in the new work and is not exhibiting outward signs of having a poor attitude, the students who will benefit will likely not know the difference. This fact is critical and must become the basis for pressing teachers into the required behaviors. Principals often work to mold the attitudes and dispositions of their staff when reluctant. To the degree that it works, it may prove to be worthwhile. However, principals will readily admit that many simply do not bring a healthy and positive attitude to the work. Leaders need to accept that they cannot change anyone's attitude, but they certainly can control how they are communicating their attitude. Teachers do not have to like the directive that a principal gives, but they do not have the luxury of rolling their eyes or making a disparaging comment.

A principal must respond to the way in which teachers choose to express their feelings. When principals respond successfully to teachers who are giving the appearance of disdain toward the work, teachers then become engaged in the work and the students have no knowledge of their personal opinions about it. When this happens, students will not be able to tell the difference between the converted, convinced, and the contained. If a teacher has cooperated in adopting the appropriate behavior, the principal simply needs to remain vigilant that the teacher is not sabotaging the work with a poor attitude.

Much like a nurse administering a vaccination to a patient, the benefit to the patient in no way depends on her faith in the potency of the medicine or her cheerfulness about injecting it. The patient benefits regardless and in spite of the nurse's belief system. Ideally, of course, this would not be an issue, but principals must do everything in their power to ensure that all students are receiving the same treatment.

While it could be argued whether all students are actually benefiting to the same degree as their peers being taught by a converted teacher, it is inarguable that the students will benefit more by a strong instructional strategy being presented by a reluctant teacher than if they did not receive the instructional strategy at all. Principals must remember that it is the experience of the student that dictates the level of response by the principal. If forcing a teacher to comply is the only way for a student to receive sound instruction, that is always preferable than a happier teacher who is engaging in poor instruction.

Left on its own, a school system will operate in a morally neutral way. That is, people will implement existing rules and procedures in a way that has been the historic practice. Hopefully, the procedures a school follows benefits students, but there may be some students who need more than the system automatically supplies. This is where well-intentioned people are called to question past practices and suggest newer ones that may serve more students in a better way.

As society evolves and students present new needs to educators, teachers must be prepared to evolve with it. Principals must send clear messages that the expectations of teachers to change their practices to help students will be the one constant in modern education. Obviously, leaders should not seek to change the behaviors of teachers for no reason, but leaders will likely seek change repeatedly if the needs of students demand it. Teachers, for their part, must be ready to respond and move from a reluctant response to the new demands of the work.

Once again, it is important to refrain from casting teachers into the roles of good guys and bad guys. People are complex in many ways and they are complex in the reasons they remain or move from their reluctance to adopt new practices. In fact, rarely do teachers fall into neat categories regardless of the issue. While one issue may convert some teachers, those very teachers may only be convinced on another issue. Those who are dedicated to the underlying cause of one idea may be unable to muster much emotional fervor for another topic.

This fact is true for everyone. The only time it creates a true dilemma in the professional setting is when the leader believes that the topic is so important that everyone must be committed. In these moments, the talents of the leader will certainly be called upon to deliver a message with sufficient heart to convert as many teachers as possible, with sound logic and rationale to convince another group, and with such clarity of expectation that those who remain unmoved will understand exactly what they must do despite their reluctance to meet their obligations.

Chapter 7

Enlisting Others into Shared Leadership

When a principal begins to increase visibility and engage in instructional conversations at new levels, it is for the purpose of bringing pride of place back to the quality of instruction in the building. As the principal began to witness exceptional practices, they sought ways in which those teachers could open up a professional dialogue with peers who were struggling with their own. These are solid steps in shoring up instructional cracks in the school's foundation. However, principals who seek to transform the educational environment within their school must also reach out to others in the spirit of shared leadership.

Unfortunately, educators have often viewed leadership too narrowly, associating it with the positional power of those with lofty job titles. This fails to seize upon a very important and often untapped aspect of leadership within the school environment. Leaders must reflect on the current status of leadership at all levels within their school and assess who takes on leadership roles, how were they recruited, and who is a source of untapped competence within the setting that may be a powerful force of change among their peers.

Once principals have analyzed the status of teacher leadership in their building, they must develop a concrete plan to bring these new voices into a shared leadership experience. This must be done with a thoughtful execution of a well-designed plan. Proper planning is essential primarily because the principal is seeking to recruit a very busy teacher into assuming new responsibilities within the system. Of course, all teachers are extremely busy and a principal must take steps not to overwhelm them with the prospect of more work.

One way to do this is by noting that this different work is important to both students and building their own professional capacity, seeing this work as an investment in themselves. However, a principal must constantly be aware that the fundamental reason teachers have chosen their profession is to teach children. Helping them see the wisdom and merit of expending any amount of time even partially removed from that work may take some coaxing. This reluctance should not be seen as a weakness; rather, it is a testament to the commitment they have to their primary job duties.

Some teachers simply have not conceived what it would look like to engage in leadership activities within their school. Their understanding of what a principal has in mind for them could be very different from what they may imagine. Therefore, principals need to move slowly and deliberately in discussing the possibility of taking larger leadership roles within the school. Many strong, potential leaders become frightened away from assisting in this work because the principal failed to communicate the reasons they should engage in this work and how they may be able to assist in ways that feel appropriate and natural.

One common misstep that principals make is to assume that teacher leaders seek to become administrators themselves. Whether teachers seek to become a principal themselves eventually, principals must recognize that teacher leadership is fundamentally distinct from an administrative leader. When a principal attempts to recruit teachers into a leadership role, both the principal and the teacher must be very clear what the work entails and how it differs from an administrative role.

Principals, for their part, must critically analyze their own intentions in promoting teacher leaders. If principals are attempting to build the capacity of teaching in their schools, this work is appropriate. If, however, principals are seeking someone to share the administrative workload (even as it relates to instruction), the plan is destined to fail. Building teacher leaders has very little to do with sharing a workload and far more to do with investing in teachers in a new way to broaden their skills in influencing others.

Principals also must reflect on which teachers come to mind as those with leadership potential. Likely, the principal will gravitate toward those who have aspirations of transitioning into administrative roles eventually. As noted, principals must be very careful not to thrust these people into roles outside of their teaching position. However, these people should not be disregarded completely either. Teachers who show interest in assuming leadership positions are a sure source of potential in identifying teacher leaders. Principals simply must take care that these teachers do not become overzealous in their attempts to evolve professionally.

Leaders may also make the short-sighted mistake of identifying teachers who remind leaders of themselves. Principals who are thriving in their position come to recognize the traits within themselves that have brought them success. It becomes very easy to associate those particular qualities as being the preferable set of qualities for a leader to possess. However, successful leaders often exhibit vastly different qualities from each other. In fact, two successful principals may exhibit leadership traits on the complete opposite end of the spectrum from each other and yet both still find a path to success. The best teacher leaders will not necessarily be the ones who remind leaders of themselves. Failing to notice and embrace the potential in those who have a different leadership style is to miss many possible opportunities to grow leaders in a building.

When principals begin to view teachers as having potential to assume leadership roles as a teacher, the principal must acknowledge that the focus of the work needs to be on classroom-level activities and the teacher's associated expertise. Principals have a very wide view of an entire school system and must balance and focus attention to an incredibly wide and diverse set of responsibilities. Recruiting teachers into leadership opportunities demands the exact opposite approach. With these teachers, principals should begin with a very narrow slice of work for a teacher to focus upon in order to grow their leadership capacity.

If the principal is the general overseeing the entire battlefield, the teacher leader is a sergeant in the trench. Rather than asking the teacher to join the principal in the war room distant from the battlefield, the principal needs to jump into the trench with the teacher.

This is not to say that being in the trenches requires the principal doing the work of the teacher. This is not what teachers need, nor is it the appropriate role for a principal to attempt. Principals should not do the work of the teacher, but like a general's understanding of the troops in the field, they should be close enough to the meaningful work to ensure that it is very well understood.

In the military, both generals and sergeants perform specific leadership functions. There are a number of aspects of this multitiered leadership model that work extremely well. Primarily, someone with leadership responsibilities must oversee the complexity of the entire system. In a complex environment, each person and group has an effect on others. This creates an environment that is, by nature, interdependent. Each individual is dependent on all others in differing ways, and the principal must ensure that the environment is healthy and productive.

Principals must pay attention to the way in which the moving pieces interact with each other and ensure the system is not negatively affected by others within. Not only does the principal need to understand what is happening in each area of the system, but they also must guide the other leaders within each area to assist with specific needs and challenges. While it is true that the general does have more positional power than the sergeant, the leadership role for the sergeant is critical as well. Ground-level troops need and depend upon their sergeant because the work of the sergeant most closely resembles their own. Certainly, the analogy falls apart in that teacher leaders are not in command of their peers. However, despite this difference, they do have the ability to exert influence, if not power, over others. To this degree, the comparison holds true. Teachers will most certainly look to their teacher leader peer for insight, guidance, and direction.

For their part, the teacher leader relies and trusts that the principal does indeed have control of the vision that is the bigger picture beyond the teacher's purview. In turn, the principal keeps in close contact with those in the trenches, collecting feedback and providing resources when necessary without micromanaging the environment. Having a layer of leadership among teachers brings assistance, insight, and efficiency in quickly understanding the dynamics of rapidly changing environments.

Historically, some teachers naturally emerge within the environment and seek to attain an informal position of leadership within the teacher ranks. Often, senior members of a faculty assume positions of authority within a school even if they have not been given an actual set of duties. Because principals often defer and acquiesce to the strong opinions of those whose tenure may be the longest, positions of power often develop without the principal's knowledge or blessing.

Principals should pay attention to all ideas and suggestions that come their way, but should also ensure that they are not making decisions simply because it is the will of someone with seniority in the building. Likewise, another source of coopted authority can emerge simply because some teachers are pushy. Every environment has a wide range of personality types and a school is no exception. Principals must be on guard against the loud and more assertive voices within a faculty. Do these voices hold sway simply because they are vocal? Often, wiser but quieter voices demure in the presence of a more aggressive peer. Without careful consideration, principals can mistake these dominant, solitary voices for the will of the group. Loud voices should not necessarily prevail. The voices with the best ideas should prevail. Principals must keep those who have pushed their way into apparent leadership roles in check lest their agenda eclipse the will of the principal or the group at large.

At other times, principals have actually created leadership positions that persist independent of a strong teacher leader to fill the role. For example, the artificial construct of lead teacher and department chair are positions that exist and persist within the building whether or not a true leader fills the role. If a principal has inherited a slate of department chairs, full consideration must be given whether to continue with the current person in that position. Since the principal is the building leader, it is absolutely the role and prerogative of that leader to place others in leadership positions as needs may dictate.

While a principal certainly owes their lead teachers or department chairs an honest conversation if they intend to change directions, the principal must be very clear that they need to select their own teacher leaders for these roles and not feel compelled to continue down a previous leader's path. Because these are established roles within the school, many teachers will defer to those in these roles without much thought or reflection. This can be very problematic if the figurehead of teacher leadership does not embody the qualities that the building leader prizes. Seeing an inferior teacher in a leadership role tarnishes the building leader's reputation in the eyes of the faculty. Teachers will certainly not trust or be inspired by a leader who chooses (or retains) weak teachers in the very few and select teacher-level leadership positions in the building. Likewise, when leaders carefully select and promote the best qualities of leadership in these positions, teachers will receive an equally strong message in the characteristics that are valued in the school system.

Principals should not let leaders assume informal positions of influence without their approval. Similarly, department chairs and lead teachers should be selected carefully with prescribed duties and limitations. While there may be a necessary purpose to having a lead teacher and department chairs within the building, none of these types of leaders capitalize on the most powerful types of leadership that can be fostered by the principal. The teacher leaders who will be of the most professional consequence and influence within a school must be selected and nurtured by the principal to fill very specific instructional roles.

Principals certainly can look to high-functioning teachers within the school to recruit new people into leadership positions. This can be done by reviewing the thoughtful categories of teachers that principals have made grouping teachers by skill set. Reviewing these lists may indeed provide a principal with some new ideas on how to cultivate potential leaders. However, a principal can also identify potential leaders by taking another approach.

Instead of relying upon those who are highly accomplished in a given skill, a leader can also choose to identify teachers who are particularly adept at solving the problems that seem to plague others in the system. Teachers seem to have similar issues that crop up repeatedly as problematic aspects of their jobs. Principals should pay close attention to the type of frustrations that seem to get mentioned repeatedly and begin to make systematic list of those issues.

One useful exercise a principal can conduct with staff is to produce a handout for staff soliciting input on aspects of their job that is particularly problematic or frustrating. This first step can be quite therapeutic for teachers as they are allowed to put a voice to an aspect of their job that is troubling them. However, principals must seek additional information before collecting this input. Principals need to require teachers to list the people within the system who are most able to solve the problem. With this step, teachers usually have no problem externalizing possible remedies to the problem.

For example, if a teacher has cited excessive absences as a problem in the school, they will likely suggest that the principal should take larger disciplinary measures against the students, a guidance counselors could meet with the student, or that a truancy officer could conduct a home visit to intervene. Each of these proposed solutions may indeed be helpful, but they are obviously displacing the solution to others.

Leaders should also ask teachers to engage in one last step in this exercise by requesting that teachers also list one constructive step they could take to advance the problem toward a solution. This brings personal ownership to the problem that has been voiced and provides a comprehensive list of those who may be helpful in bringing these problems to a better place. This exercise is extremely helpful in problem-solving emerging frustrations within a school setting, but it is also a way that principals can begin considering who may be solving these difficult problems on their own.

By digging deeper into researching who solves the problems that seem to plague others, principals may identify a potential leader. When a teacher is capable of solving a difficult issue that peers find insurmountable, there is incredible promise in digger deeper into that teacher's mind-set and abilities. Some teachers become paralyzed when faced with a stumbling block; others react with frustration or despair. Conversely, when yet another set of teachers are faced with the exact same circumstance and invest themselves in working toward a productive solution, principals must recognize the potential in nurturing them as leaders.

School systems can often feel like giant cruise ships on the ocean. They are large and complex and move in their current direction through a combination of momentum and habitual force. If the cruise ship is heading in the proper direction, it can be a powerful and effective force for good that can withstand rough seas and much adversity. However, if the ship is off course to any degree, it is not particularly easy to get the ship turned in a new direction. In contrast, a teacher who has tackled a perennial problem in the school is like a speed boat. The speed boat does not have many of the qualities of a cruise ship but does have the distinct advantage of being fast and nimble. The speed boat is able to make instantaneous course corrections and can maneuver adeptly in rapidly changing circumstances. These problem-solving teachers function in the same agile manner as the speed boat. They can provide needed contrast to the sluggish cruise ship and point to new ways of approaching problems and frustrations within the environment.

For example, a narrative can easily begin to take hold in a school that the students are lazy and apathetic. Before long, this is the story that teachers tell in explaining why students are not completing their work. In time, many teachers continue to express their frustration that students do not complete their work, but express the problem as a fatalistic and inherent flaw with their group of students. Combatting this narrative can be a daunting task for a principal.

When the principal hears the narrative about students refusing to do work, the leaders should press the teacher for specific names of students who are emblematic of the problem. Next, the principal should simply begin noting which teachers do not have missing work showing up in their gradebooks. Through some simple cross-referencing, the principal will soon find students who are not completing work in some classes but are having no problems in another class. The principal must immediately seek out the teacher who is able to capture work from these supposed lazy students. Without mentioning names of their peers, the principal should interview these teachers and ascertain the reasons why they are not having the problem. By pressing them for specific techniques they use, they may begin to see the methods they use that are not being used elsewhere. Often, the teacher may not be able to articulate fully the reasons for their success. The principal should visit her classroom, keying upon the struggling students and noting why their behavior seems to be more productive in one place than another. Likewise, the principal should compliment the students for their success in the class and inquire why they are doing so much better in one class than another.

Ultimately, the principal is going to establish a handful of teachers who are able to solve problems that their peers cannot. Because frustrated teachers truly desire a remedy to their struggles, the principal should urge the successful teacher to extend their efforts and to discuss their approaches with others. Not only is there a powerful and practical reason for tapping into the expertise of those who are problem solvers, there is a profound psychological element to recruiting them. Teachers who have found success where others have struggled immediately disprove false narratives in the building. Struggling teachers can no longer take issue with a principal's urging that solutions are possible. Rather, they can focus on a peer who has successfully conquered the source of frustration. This gives an instant credibility to the teacher and can build momentum for them to be seen as more than a peer. This can be the preliminary stages of developing a fledgling teacher leader.

Through this systematic process of collecting teacher frustrations and finding bright spots in the environment, principals may both efficiently solve problems and groom new leaders in their building. However, this is not the only way potential leaders can be inspired to take on new roles. Sometimes teachers can only find a new voice of leadership when they are moved away from their typical peer group. Whether it is within grade-level teams at an elementary or within a department at a secondary school, teachers establish a niche where they spend most of their time. While learning to collaborate with those closest to others is critical in developing strong teams within a school, it can stagnate thinking and discussions over the course of time.

Each teacher tends to find their own role within a team and struggles to interact in ways that are not typical and expected. In time, teams may begin to function smoothly, but individuals may fall into a rut and fail to push themselves beyond ways in which they normally function. This creates a team culture that may be maximized based on the limits of each member's contribution but no longer has a catalyst to transform anyone's thinking.

With this approach, art teachers work with art teachers and science teachers work with science teachers. Imagine how each of these teams could become re-energized if a principal were to select an art teacher and a science teacher to join together to discuss their disciplines. For example, suppose a principal asked the following question to the art teacher, "How would you describe the science behind teaching art?" Likewise, the principal could ask the science teacher, "How would you describe the art of teaching science?" Asking these two teachers to step out of their usual thinking in each other's presence is likely to create a dynamic and intriguing conversation.

Each may struggle at first to use the vocabulary and imagery of the other's area of expertise. As the principal guides the conversation, each teacher could then weigh in on how the other may view their own discipline differently by considering it from each other's vantage point. When science teachers get together to discuss their content area, they probably don't think too much about how their discipline might be thought of in creative terms. An art teacher could assist in this sort of thinking. While it may not be possible to predict what sort of value may emerge from this conversation, intelligent and thoughtful people thinking about their work in novel ways usually produce powerful work. When science teachers are challenged to conceive of their work in this different sort of way, they may then return to their usual conversations with their science peers with a fresh and altered perspective. This can infuse new possibilities that can grow stale without outside influence.

Principals should consider how they may best recombine groups to encourage this sort of cross-pollination in thinking among their staff. These recombined groups can be formed in countless ways. Sometimes, principals may desire to form new thinking groups based upon concrete topics such as parent involvement or student engagement. Other times, principals may stimulate new thinking by addressing more philosophical concepts such as the meaning of rigor in classrooms.

Groups that are recombined create hybrid thinking. Hybrid thinking allows for ideas that cross over from the typical parallel lines of thinking that emerge from like-minded people working together. When opportunities for hybrid thinking are designed and encouraged, principals often see new types of leaders emerge. Teachers may be content to follow when they are running with their normal pack but may emerge as powerful frontrunners in newly conceived territory. The role of the leader is to create these spaces so hybrid thinking can be fostered. Of course, this sort of experimentation can seem a bit odd for professionals who have worked in traditional environments.

Principals may need to be prepared to carry the conversation and model it for a time until a common language develops in these unique groupings. Quite simply, art teachers view and speak about the world in an entirely different vocabulary than their scientific peers. Creating a common space where each side is not quick to dismiss the other's world view can take some time and patience. Science teachers must be convinced that the point is not to morph them into an art teacher, but rather to understand that they may be better science teachers if they look at their discipline from a fresh angle.

One does not have to look far to see how powerful recombined ideas have transformed society. The motor and carriage existed in parallel in the late 1800s. When they were combined, the resulting automobile not only redefined the significance of each component but also created a new concept that has become more consequential than the two inventions considered separately. Educators must constantly probe the ways in which their thinking can be recombined to conceive of better ideas than the sum of the individuals' thoughts. Not every teacher will excel in this progressive work. However, those who do embrace the potential of these new conversations are yet another source of teacher leaders within the school.

The power of these hybrid thinkers is that they are not just likely to produce better ideas, but also they are the ones who will conceive of new ideas. Principals should not limit their own conception of teacher leaders as "the best" of each type of teacher. Considering a new stable of leaders as a collection of simply the best science teacher, the best math teacher, and the best language arts teacher is too simplistic and misses the larger point of developing new leaders. Aside from content and grade-level experts, *thought* leaders on a wide range of topics can become powerful teacher leaders.

Unfortunately, teachers seem to be conditioned to believe that problems and frustrations in the school setting are inevitable. Because so many issues seem to reoccur over time and across different schools, teachers may begin to believe that many difficulties must be suffered and endured rather than systematically addressed and solved. Indeed, many problems do persist within schools and can give the appearance that they are without remedy. Otherwise, teachers would not fall into this sort of pessimism. The difference is that some leaders refuse to take this fatalistic view of the problems that plague educators and build strong systems to implement solutions.

The guidance of teacher leaders is one level of leadership that increases the likelihood that this will happen. However, even strong teachers may not have the perspective and understanding to implement any of their great practices without the guidance of a building leader to point the way. Many teachers have strong capacity to bring about great work but need the leader to unlock that potential with encouragement and support. In the following scenario, the principal morphs the frustration of Ms. Rivera into a new opportunity for both her and their school.

Teacher: "Thanks for making time for me today. I know you're busy but I am very frustrated and hope you can hear me out."

Principal: "Absolutely. What is on your mind?"

Teacher: "Well, it is the new state exam for our kids. Have you looked very closely at it?"

Principal: "I have read a number of the press releases from the department of education and have looked at their talking points on their website."

Teacher: "But aside from all of that, have you actually looked at the released test items for sixth grade in math?"

Principal: "No, I must admit that I haven't. What are you seeing?"

Teacher: "It's not good. There are a number of concepts that our current textbook doesn't even cover. Others only have a couple of lessons."

Principal: "That is a problem."

Teacher: "With all due respect, you know my partner teachers are doing nothing other than page by page in their text. They are not omitting or supplementing lessons. For every teacher who does it that way, we are going to have entire groups of kids who do not even learn many of the things that will be on their state exam."

Principal: "Can we adjust the pacing guide for sixth-grade math?"

Teacher: "It's just not that simple. There are concepts that require double the time and some that we should shrink considerably. It's not just the number of concepts that is shocking, but the numbers of questions for each of them is different from what I thought."

Principal: "I'm not sure I'm following you."

Teacher: "Look right here. It says ten out of the fifty-seven questions on the math exam will be focused on geometry."

Principal: "That seems like a lot. How does it compare to the old exam?"

Teacher: "Probably double the amount. But it gets worse. Our current pacing guide has us teaching most of it in the weeks after the exam date."

Principal: "They won't have even been exposed to nearly 10 percent of the entire exam?"

Teacher: "That's right. Do you see why I am freaking out?"

Principal: "Ms. Rivera, I cannot thank you enough for recognizing this problem. We need to address this. Will you help me?"

Teacher: "What do you mean?"

Principal: "I have not heard anyone else across the city talking about this. You have an incredible head start in understanding the extent of the problem. Will you work with me to map this out so we can see the entirety of the issue and look for ways to realign our current pacing guides? If we can stay nine weeks ahead of the teachers, it won't interfere much with their lesson design, will it?"

Teacher: "No, I don't think anyone can plan more than a few weeks ahead since we have to adapt to how our students are progressing. But they will freak out knowing that we are only staying a few weeks ahead of them."

Principal: "I think you are mistaken, Ms. Rivera. I think your colleagues are going to recognize that you know more than anyone about the intricacies of the state exam and will appreciate your insight and leadership on this."

Teacher: "Oh man, I don't know. This isn't really my area of expertise. I understand the pacing guides, but I haven't ever written one."

Principal: "Well, we can work on it together. Keep in mind that we are readjusting it, not starting from scratch. In less than five minutes, you've convinced me of the problem and how we need to change our focus."

Teacher: "Can I set aside the next professional planning session we have scheduled to start laying this out?"

Principal: "Certainly, we can use my conference room. I'll block off my schedule and bring in lunch. Let me know if you need any supplies or copies or anything. Let's do this."

Ms. Rivera is a talented teacher who uncovered a critical flaw in her school's curriculum pacing guide. Initially, the passion and intensity she brought to the conversation was focused on convincing the principal of the extent of the problem. The principal immediately recognized that her assessment of the new state exam was accurate and that they were indeed faced with a problem. Rather than resigning the kids of their school to unfair preparation for an important exam, the principal saw the opportunity of transforming the teacher's expertise in discovering the problem into the possibility of solving it. The leader was quick to recognize she was the person with the requisite skills to solve this problem and was likely able to do so with some reassurance that she is capable. The principal accommodated her potential needs by providing the time and resources to accomplish the work. Importantly, the principal immediately agreed to block time in the calendar to assist.

Problems can be inevitable in the complex world of education. A principal's thoughtful response to the problem can not only solve them as they come, but can also build leaders through the process. In this scenario, the problem will undoubtedly be resolved, and the skill set of this astute teacher will be sharpened and refined. As the changes are communicated to her peers, they will certainly begin relying on her as a teacher leader on other important instructional issues.

Offering sufficient support for teachers who are trying to extend themselves into new roles is a critical requirement for success. Teachers often feel like they lack adequate resources to complete their primary tasks as teachers. Schools where teachers are forced to utilize their own funds in order to buy basic supplies for the classroom are certainly at a disadvantage in supporting teachers in all aspects of their work. Principals in these situations should conduct a fundamental auditing of their expenditures to ensure that sums of money are not leaking out of the system in inefficient or unnecessary ways.

Most principals retain line items within their budget for professional development and some of these dollars should be reserved to support teachers trying to grow as professionals. Likewise, principals should make a strong plea to district-level leaders to support the professional growth of teachers through earmarked federal dollars, which are specifically set aside to support professional development. Becoming knowledgeable of all available pots of money is critical for a principal trying to support robust work with limited funds.

These funds can be used in a number of ways. Teacher who have the potential to become teacher leaders are often those who already invest heavily in themselves as professionals. These are the teachers who have bookshelves full of books about their profession and are the first to look for additional resources to help them grow. In the big picture of a school's overall budget, setting aside some funds to support a teacher's book habit is always a sound investment.

Often, educators will attend a lengthy and expensive professional development conference costing thousands of dollars only to conclude that the keynote speaker merely rehashed their latest book. Suppose instead that the principal rerouted those thousands of dollars and spent them instead on a mini-budget to support the topics being embraced by teacher leaders in the building. Thirty new books on the shelf of a teacher would probably transform their attitude and practices about growing as a professional. The cost of these thirty books would probably be less than the hotel costs of the next planned conference. By having teachers engage in a book study, the learning of a book can be deeply contemplated and internalized by everyone studying the text and will not be forgotten after memories of a conference quickly fade.

Investing in teachers attending a conference should not be seen necessarily as a waste of money, however. These conferences often are wasteful, but that need not be the case. The reason why conferences are met with a suspicious eye has more to do than just the appealing vacation destination spot where most of them are located. Principals should be skeptical of supporting conferences if their topic and need are not clearly established. If the conference is focused on the next steps that teachers need to learn in order to advance their practice, they are often the best investment that can be made for a school.

If a conference is worth supporting, a principal should commit themself to attending the event with a team. This brings focus to the work and ensures that attendees treat it as the professional investment that it should be rather than a glorified vacation on the taxpayers' dime. Conferences usually end early enough each day where attendees can enjoy a bit of what the location has to offer. Principals should not be too quick to release teachers into the city at the conclusion of each day's itinerary.

Instead, principals should require their team to gather for one hour at the conclusion of each day to debrief on the day's learning. By asking all participants to reflect on the learning and commit to new practices in light of what they have learned, a principal can anchor their new learning back to new practices upon their return to school. Because teachers are usually away from home, these professional conversations are very productive as these busy individuals can devote their undivided attention to professional dialogue that may otherwise be impossible due to thousands of daily distractions.

Principals should be mindful that the conversations they engage in with these teachers should include their current responsibilities but should also stretch into the new demands that a principal is trying to build within the blossoming teacher leader. Allowing them to grow to meet their current professional challenges as well as supporting them in new work honors both their present professional focus and their potential.

The kind of support teachers may require as they stretch themselves to become teacher leaders may take a variety of forms. Primarily, any new work teachers are asked to assume requires time in order to accomplish it. Because principals are no longer themselves tied to a classroom for predetermined lengths of time, they often forget that teachers are bound to their classrooms supervising and teaching groups of students for most of their contract day. A lack of available blocks of time is certainly a fundamental constraint on how principals may be able to ask teachers to devote efforts to new work.

One way to address this is to hire a substitute teacher and allow the teacher leader to dedicate time during the school day to focus on new tasks. While this is convenient, the principal must be very prudent in taking this approach as the quality of classroom is always negatively impacted when a teacher is absent. However, at times a principal may decide this is a worthwhile investment. If eight hours of innovative thinking and work product are produced, it may be indeed worth having a teacher leave the classroom in another's hands.

This is also helpful to teachers as it does not add hours to their day asking them to be gone from their family commitments to take part in additional work. Not only is this a strain on a teacher's priorities, but it also can drain a teacher's limited reserves of energy.

A principal may also invest in a teachers' leadership development by giving them a place in decision-making meetings beyond their normal scope of duties. For example, in the scenario described earlier, the principal may make an arrangement for Ms. Rivera to participate in an upcoming district-level academic council meeting to discuss her findings. The positive response she is sure to receive from a wider audience may awaken a desire to spread her circle of influence beyond its current dimensions within her school. A principal can assist the process of helping teachers see themselves in new ways by supporting them in these moments that build their professional credibility and capacity. Giving teachers access to levels of leadership conversations that have been formerly out of their realm is a powerful way to support a teacher's new vision of themselves.

Teachers must have a leader who will invest in them if they are to develop and emerge as potential leaders within their building. Principals who seize opportunities to attack problems within the environment by investing in teachers are on their way to building multiple leadership possibilities for their staff. When this is done well and responsibly, teachers have a new source of inspiration and support in their work. However, principals must take care that the way in which they ask teachers to assist in leadership roles is truly in a leadership capacity. If principals have been guilty of remaining in managerial roles and mistakenly believing they are leading, they are also suspect of trying to lead potential leaders into managerial roles as well.

For example, in Ms. Rivera's case, the principal could easily make a mistake in asking her to produce a written report that is then forwarded along to others. If this were to be the approach, the principal has relegated her powerful insight into a clerical role. The problem she identified does not need to be memorialized on paper, but it needs discussed and debated. The issue demands thoughtful problem-solving and a clear method of communicating the complexities of the problem with others.

When principals position potential leaders on leadership committees, these teachers are often saddled with paperwork and required reporting rather than reserving their contribution to leadership tasks. Principals should ask administrative assistants to join a meeting if there are required reports or plans that need produced. Asking teachers to assume leadership roles while tasking them with formatting and producing documents is a waste of their talents and will surely dampen their desire to grow in new ways.

Often, it would seem that principals are more focused on the distribution of unappealing tasks and see their teacher leader peers as a way to share the burden of a heavy workload. Principals must resist this urge and seek relief elsewhere. If growing teachers as leaders is important, it must be important enough to shelter them from shuffling papers in the name of leadership. Instead, leaders must determine what the final work product will be in light of the new work that is being supported by the teachers. Maintaining the focus on a high-quality work product that is only able to be produced by the work of leaders within the trenches is the way to guarantee that emerging teacher leaders will truly be developing as leaders themselves.

The principal must clearly define the role for teacher leaders. The work must be progressive but yet appropriate at the same time. Teachers are not administrators. Likely, they do not wish to be a principal or even to be seen as a pseudo-principals. The new space that a principal seeks to cultivate for teacher leaders must remain a safe place for them to operate. The space does not become unsafe because they are engaging in powerful and innovative work that is different from their peers. Rather, the space becomes unsafe when the way the work that is framed alienates teachers from their peers. Students are not the only group of individuals fond of the term "teacher's pet." This term is coopted by teachers every day to describe the teacher who somehow seems to have an inside track with a superior.

Teachers are very sensitive to whether one of their own is risen to a new place of prominence. While developing as a teacher leader is certainly a noble and worthy way for a teacher to evolve professionally, it should not be looked at as having teachers occupy a place of prominence. Quite the contrary, it should be viewed the same as the principal who engages in meaningful work. It is not a place of distinction, but it is a place squarely in the trenches of education.

The difference is found in the new conversations and work that emerge from the most difficult environment that the professional of education has to offer. From start to finish, both principals and teacher leaders must be transparent that their work is meant to help everyone understand the difficulties of the profession and bring frustrating work to a better place. To do anything less will create an environment where teachers resent both the principal and those who are taking a risk by trying to exercise some leadership qualities.

Principals can do many things to assist in making the healthiness of this work more apparent. First, the principal must make it very clear that the teachers being brought into this work are primarily leading work, not their peers. Teachers will resent the idea that their coworker is now somehow, by administrative fiat, in charge of them. Teachers do not need another boss, they need fellow coworkers who have the courage and will to lead important work.

One fundamental caution for principals is that they must never put teachers in a position where they are asked to report negatively upon their peers. If there is a behavior that a principal needs to witness, that principal should go witness it firsthand rather than putting teachers in the role of confidential informant. If fellow teachers get the sense that working with a principal comes at the price of the principal pumping them for information about their peers, the trust of the entire building will collapse in upon itself. Principals must realize that they may need to step back a bit and let teachers work more independently than this joint effort in leadership may suggest. Teachers who are grappling with perennial problems in their setting need the support of a principal, not the continual presence of the principal over their shoulder in the work. Principals must have enough situational awareness to recognize which conversations require their absence as much as which conversations demand their presence.

Teacher leaders need to grow in their role. One way to help them grow is to make sure they are not planted in the shadow of the building leader. Teachers can thrive in their new role without constant supervision. Principals must be situational leaders. There will be times when the principal needs to serve as a resource provider only. In those moments, the leader must be dedicated to finding those resources even under scarce conditions. At other times, teacher leaders may need a sounding board to listen to their frustrations and anxieties about the uncertainty of this new work and their role in it. In these moments, principals need to be careful listeners to make sure the teachers are understood. Of course, there will be times when the teacher leaders will come to the principal needing a fellow thought partner. When these occasions arise, principals must be prepared to roll up their sleeves and get as deep into the work as their teachers need them to be.

Chapter 8

Creating Productive Space within the Trench

The actual presence that principals have in the classroom is directly related to how important they view this work and their level of commitment to being present in that space. With that said, the actual interaction principals have will undoubtedly wax and wane as relationships are built or weakened and in accordance to the rhythms of the school year. The kind of work teachers can attempt when they are refreshed and focused may be different from the work that is possible after long, difficult stretches of instruction as the school year plays out.

Hopefully, principals will renew their commitment to having a presence within classrooms. Beyond simply becoming more visible in classrooms, principals can operate on an entire spectrum of engagement in schools. Aside from being more present, principals can choose to become careful observers of the environment, noticing patterns of strengths and weaknesses in the instructional delivery. A further commitment is shown by engaging in dialogue with teachers to discuss and problem solve ongoing frustrations and dilemmas that plague dedicated teachers.

In addition, principals can support the particular interests of those teachers who seek to move their understanding deeper. Engaging with these teachers in a way that promotes their ability to serve as teacher leaders for their peers is one of the highest functions a principal can serve. However, even if a principal commits to operating on this furthest cutting edge of leadership, it will become immediately clear that the entire leadership approach hinges upon the professional quality and commitment of the people within the system. Some principals will be blessed to operate in a setting where there is no shortage of talent and desire to grow as a professional and engage in meaningful conversations about instruction. Teachers in these settings long for an instructional leader who will value their professional contribution and grow as fast as the leader will allow.

However, not all schools will have a staff that has this sort of capacity at any given moment. In some schools, principals may feel like personnel who are willing to commit to new conversations and new work seems scarce. In these situations, principals must analyze the discrepancy between the current and desired level of performance. This should not be the sort of reality check that causes a principal to downshift expectations and refrain from pushing the staff toward a higher instructional ideal. Instead, principals must commit to building stronger structures and systems that grow the capacity of their teachers.

Thus far, principals have created a presence that results in an intersection between themselves and teachers who were poised to take their work deeper. The techniques a principal should employ are strategies to capitalize on an opportunity that currently exists. Up to this point, the principal may not have been aware that there was work ripening under their noses with curious and tenacious teachers who are driven to improve instruction. Moving these teachers along in their work is essential but can be managed in many ways simply by acknowledging and supporting the work they were contemplating anyway.

With other staff members, principals need to create events and occasions where others may come to similar realization but thus far, have not. Without creating a definite plan to cause others to have an instructional awakening, many potentially strong teacher leaders may not have a moment of clarity where they recognize that they too are ready to begin new work. Without instituting concrete structures to encourage this work, the system will only ever be as strong as the collection of individuals and their present interests and pursuits. Schools can and should be stronger than the sum of their collective members. However, this does not accidentally happen. Schools can indeed function beyond the sum of its parts when people are supported by strong structures and systems that are not dependent on the present skills and will of the members.

Creating deliberate structures that value and inspire best practices and conversations around them is the only way to guarantee that every staff member is sure to have an encounter with the challenge of adopting better work. In the absence of these strong systems, principals must acknowledge that the prospect of teachers elevating their practice may only be as likely as the good fortune of the principal stumbling onto an interesting conversation that catches the teacher's attention sparking a lively discussion. Limiting the work to these occasions is certainly better than nothing but leaves too much to chance and coincidence.

The structures that a principal builds into the daily operation of the system can take many forms. However, the purpose for each is the same. The principal must develop accessible opportunities within the building that model the desired outcomes for all students in the school. When structures are put in place where teachers can see these best instructional practices and then engage in meaningful conversation and debate around this work, the system creates and replicates opportunities for teachers to engage.

Developing multiple on-ramps for teachers to enter into deeper professional conversations acknowledges that many teachers with strong potential may be *close* to adopting new practices but are not quite there. Creating scaffolded opportunities to engage with others around progressive work is the best opportunity to create a safe yet challenging environment that can push the thinking of professionals in a healthy way. Teachers who are ready to take on new challenges will likely respond to the prompting and support of a principal acting as an instructional leader. Others may have incredible potential but opt out because they remain a bit intimidated to take an official step forward. Yet, in a controlled environment where smaller steps are encouraged while being supported by the work of a larger group, they may creep more closely toward a place where they are able to take bolder steps when approached. Therefore, principals must create deliberate structures that encourage and promote the type of thinking that can serve as a nursery for those who need to mature in their thinking and confidence in order to take their next professional steps.

One of the most widely adopted structures in place at many schools is the formation of collaborative team meetings. The form and structure of these meetings may vary a bit depending on the school of thought where educators have received their training, but the fundamental premise is the same. With this model, teacher teams meet on a regular basis to review student performance on collaboratively developed assessments. In light of student performance, teachers then discuss how they will respond instructionally. While this approach seems very straightforward and has been widely adopted across the country, most schools continue to struggle with authentic implementation of this process in a consistent and reliable manner.

Although countless staff developers have articulated each of the necessary steps in accomplishing this work, teacher teams usually struggle with full implementation. There is great promise with this model in promoting best instructional practices as well as developing teacher leaders through the process. Unfortunately, teams often lose their way in this process getting derailed for various reasons. One primary reason why teams struggle is that some team members believe that they have successfully engaged in this work if several professionals sit in the same room and discuss school-related topics. This may be a good start, but authentic collaboration demands more than generalized conversations about whichever topics are on the minds of teachers.

Assuming teachers stay true to the requisite steps in collaboration, teams can fall apart in other ways. Often, teachers are willing to engage in conversations about the content standards they are tasked with teaching. They can usually reach a compromise in developing a common assessment that measures those standards. It is in the next step that teachers typically falter. In examining student performance, patterns inevitably emerge. Sometimes, a group of students performs worse than a teacher anticipated, and the teacher is unsure why it happened. Similarly, some teachers have students who outperform the students of other classes, and the disparity of results creates an awkwardness among the team.

These are the moments when the teams must decide what they will do next. It is also the point at which many good teams fall apart and fail to take action. At times, this is because team members begin to blame the students and focus their attention on what the students should have done differently. This results in a team conversation that merely describes the problem students are having and fails to take ownership of how the grown-ups can intervene to bring the situation to a better place.

On other occasions, it is because teachers have a hard time admitting that different results were indeed possible and their peers have engaged in a more effective practice. Not only were other practices more beneficial but the student results bear witness to these superior practices. These moments are extremely humbling for the most dedicated educator and demand that teams put student needs beyond the embarrassment of having students underperform.

Leaders must create a strong system that clearly articulates the structure of how team meetings are expected to operate. Monitoring the function of these teams is essential to prevent the emergence of productive teams that only appear in random pockets throughout the building. Likewise, leaders must insist that the work of the team is not done until new informed decisions are made for students depending on their current levels of performance. Principals must gauge how much of a presence they must exert in order to keep these meetings functional and productive. Often, the role a principal can play in building teacher efficacy within their teams occurs outside of the team meeting offering support when a teacher is unsure how to proceed in a difficult conversation. In the following scenario, a teacher is expressing frustration in another team member who is reluctant to consider new classroom practices.

Teacher: "Do I have to work with Mr. Griffin anymore?"

Principal: "Uh oh, what's going on?"

Teacher: "He's just so frustrating. Mr. Benitez and I are really interested in using an instructional protocol on analyzing text and Mr. Griffin won't even consider it. I just wish we could meet without him."

Principal: "Sounds like you're a bit frustrated. Let me ask you, do you feel he is responding in a professional way?"

Teacher: "Yeah, I mean, he's polite and everything, but he just refuses to try things that we know will work."

Principal: "What does he want to do instead?"

Teacher: "Like always, he wants to use whatever he pulls out of his filing cabinet from fifteen years ago."

Principal: "Do you have a reading passage that you intend to use with this new protocol?"

Teacher: "Yeah, at least we have agreed to read the same passage and give the common assessment on it."

Principal: "Well, that's a start. But maybe there's another way to keep these innovative ideas in play without alienating him from your group."

Teacher: "What do you have in mind?"

Principal: "What if you proposed to the group that you will give the students the protocol on analyzing text to your students before they read the passage, Mr. Benitez will give it to the students after they read the passage, and Mr. Griffin will purposefully not use it at all. Then, after the students take the common assessment, the quality of student work will determine if the protocol is more useful and, if so, maybe it will tell you the best time to introduce it to students."

Teacher: "Well, he certainly won't object to not using it!"

Principal: "Sure, but allow him to persist in his belief until the data prove otherwise. Arguing over the merits of an instructional support that you haven't used yet is not likely to convince him. Keep him operating within the team by encouraging him to try his approach. But that needs to be the beginning of the conversation, not the end. Do you think he might be swayed by better results?"

Teacher: "Actually, I do. He has said on numerous occasions that he thinks my students are a harder group than his."

Principal: "So, make your case through the exemplary performance of your students."

The principal shows great poise in this scenario by remaining calm and patient when the teacher first approaches. Because teachers are not accustomed to healthy professional conflict, disagreement within collaborative team meetings can first appear to be the sort of disagreement that makes teachers want to flee. When teachers are frustrated in these moments, leaders must first establish that everyone continues to behave in a professional manner. Distinguishing between teachers who are being strong-willed but appropriate is an important distinction to make. When teachers are, in fact, disagreeing in an appropriate manner, principals must reassure the team that this does not signal dysfunction, but rather an opportunity to press onward in a healthy debate.

Based on the facts that were shared, there was no reason that the principal needed to become directly involved in the team debate. Rather, the frustrated teacher needed support in recognizing that the situation could be salvaged and brought to new levels of understanding by framing the message in the proper way. Persisting in these moments of frustration is not necessarily a strong suit for teachers. Quite simply, these conversations are not part of the skill set that makes them great teachers. They are, however, the very skills that make them great professional educators. Principals must remain patient as teachers work their way through these difficult professional interactions.

In addition to regular collaborative team meetings, principals must develop additional instructional structures that can build the skills of teachers and nurture their capacity as teacher leaders. Educators can benefit from looking to other professionals to find structures valued in other industries and adapt them within school settings. In the medical community, physicians have historically conducted *attending rounds* within a hospital that serves an important function in growing and developing the skills of others.

When conducting rounds, physicians assemble other doctors, residents, and associated healthcare professionals to discuss the status and care of the patient and determine best steps moving forward. These rounds are an integral part of the educational process for young physicians but also stretch and mature the thinking of the most expert physician leading the rounds. In these moments, the patient becomes the textbook. Physicians are presented with very concrete examples of those needing their care. When rounds are conducted most appropriately, ideas and plans are freely exchanged for the benefit of the patient needing care, but also for the professionals who stretch themselves in these real-world conversations about the application of best practices in medicine.

There is a direct equivalent between a physician's attending rounds and the potential practices of an educator. Principals can easily implement a system of instructional rounds that model the practices of physicians within a school setting. Of course, principals need to engage the faculty in the purpose of these rounds as the practice will demand that teams of teachers led by the principal move throughout the building visiting classrooms as they are in session. Principals need to remind teachers that these rounds are not rooted in a desire to be critical of the practices they witness.

Although the teams will likely witness both exemplary and questionable practices, the leader must remind teachers that classrooms are not closed environments outside the review and observations of educational professionals. Teachers, of course, need to be mindful that their presence within classrooms needs to remain professional and discreet so the learning environment is respected and preserved. In fact, students will quickly learn that the work they are doing in their classes is so important that others desire to observe their work in action. When handled in this fashion, instructional rounds enhance the importance of normal classroom instruction and support the engagement of students in their classes rather than distracting from the important work that should be happening.

Principals must work within the terms of their teachers' contractual planning time to conduct these instructional rounds. Leaders must work with teachers to note that designated planning time has often been left entirely to teachers as a time for them to put materials together for the next day's teaching. While teachers certainly require a measure of time to plan lessons, instructional planning time must evolve in a school to be more than just a bit of free time to make copies. It is entirely appropriate for teachers to use their designated planning times to incorporate these observational opportunities on a periodic basis.

If principals are tapping into this valuable time, it is incumbent on the leader to make these rounds valuable and productive. Teachers have very little time within their day when they are not teaching but class is in session elsewhere in the building. Principals must demand some of this time to build in opportunities for teachers to witness other instruction. In fact, most teachers have very few opportunities to witness any other teaching because they are usually working simultaneously with their peers. This results in a professional environment where teachers are surrounded by instruction but are highly unlikely to witness others engaged in instruction. Principals must change this reality by instituting instructional rounds.

Leaders must take care to frame the purpose for each set of rounds very carefully. Without careful guidance, teachers may seize upon problems or deficiencies they notice. This can increase the anxiety and reluctance for teachers to be observed and bring dysfunction into a very powerful opportunity. If a teacher witnesses nothing other than teachers being critical of other teachers practices, they will certainly recognize that the same negative scrutiny will be focused on them when teams visit their classroom. Instead, principals should be highly involved in setting the topic and tone of a well-planned set of instructional rounds. For example, a principal should decide upon a theme for teachers to notice before the rounds begin.

Rather than waiting until the conclusion of the rounds and asking what teachers thought went well, principals should prescriptively select predetermined look-fors and isolate the conversation to the selected focus area of the day. For example, a principal may decide to focus a group on ways teachers use nonlinguistic representations in the classroom. The group then briefly visits a number of classrooms examining if teachers are using instructional supports such as idea webs, concept maps, and graphic organizers to represent their thinking. This focuses those conducting the rounds so they are not trying to observe everything the class has to offer. After spending a few minutes in the classroom, they are able to debrief quickly in the hallway before moving on to the next classroom.

Principals should take great care to remind observers to note what students were doing and the work they were producing rather than focusing exclusively upon teacher actions. Depending on the occasion, principals can focus the work around innumerable instructional practices. With care, they can engage observers in what seemed to go well and what could have been done differently. Principals need to keep these conversations honest, but as positive as possible. With every visit, principals should ask each observer what implications the observations have for *their own* practice as well. The benefit of this is that it prevents the rounds from being a coordinated effort at criticizing their peers.

Another way principals can guide teachers to improve their practice is through implementing lab classrooms. This structure gives teachers the opportunity to request feedback from their peers in a strategic way. Lab classrooms are a collaborative professional development activity where one teacher serves as a host for a group of other participants. In contrast to instructional rounds, teachers take time before class to prebrief with the host on what they will be observing in class during their visit. The host takes the time to explain the purpose and intent behind their instructional decisions and invites the participants to take notes about what they notice and asks the observers to pay close attention to whatever phenomenon they are hoping to improve during that lesson.

For example, a teacher may decide that conferring with students in a meaningful way is something that the teacher has been focusing on and seeks to improve. The observers will then take special note of how successful the teacher is on this particular point of emphasis. Because the teacher spends some time prebriefing with observers beforehand, everyone is clear from the onset as to what the teacher is attempting to accomplish. Ideally, a principal begins these lab classrooms with teachers who are not necessarily experts on a given topic but are willing to open up their practice to others nonetheless.

When teachers come to observe the lab classroom, it is important that they take extensive notes around the focus of the lab classroom. While teachers may also be interested in observations apart from the area of focus, care must be taken not to derail the focus of the lab classroom. Observers are likely to interact in a more intimate way in lab classrooms than during instructional rounds as they have been invited into the thinking of the lesson. They will have all of the teacher's handouts and should be closely examining the way in which students experience the lesson.

As appropriate, lab classroom participants should interact with students, questioning them about how they are processing the work. Because participants could easily derail students from their work with too much interaction, the host teacher should establish clear protocols during the prebrief on how the teacher would like them to participate. Participants should actively collect data during the session while honoring the existing atmosphere that the teacher has created in the classroom.

After the class period, both the host and the lab classroom participants spend time together debriefing on the lesson. Participants should refrain from making judgments about what they observed but should instead describe their observations objectively. This conversation should be collaborative, not evaluative, in nature. In light of this feedback, the host should also contribute to the conversation describing what went as planned or differently than envisioned. After everyone has a chance to describe what they had observed, participants should engage in lively questioning of both the host and other participants around the focus of the lesson. This is a time for everyone to begin processing the learning and deciding what implications the conversation has for their own future practice.

By witnessing someone put theory into practice in a real-world situation, practitioners have a tangible experience of what experimentation in a classroom setting can look like. Leaders should be an integral part of these lab classrooms and should encourage a spirit of professional inquiry regarding what is possible within classrooms. Hopefully, witnessing teachers take professional risks as instructors will encourage and embolden the participants to engage in similar practices. In time, participants should be encouraged to host a lab classroom experience themselves.

It is important to note that teachers are not experts at all aspects of the job. Lab classrooms are not meant to be reserved solely for those who have reputations as expert teachers. Rather, the lab classroom is a place where honest attempts at instructional improvement are valued and developed. The environment must be trusting enough that participants do not walk away from the experience believing that marginal practices are, in fact, exemplary simply because a host focused attention on them during a lab classroom. The benefit of a lab classroom is in the deep conversations about best practices rather than mimicking what was done by another.

Leaders must recognize that lab classrooms have the added requirement of pulling teachers out of their own classrooms in order to have time to prebrief, observe, and debrief. This is certainly both a financial investment by requiring substitute teachers for a few hours and a burden upon students who will be without their regular classroom teacher for a period of time. Principals must determine if they are willing to make such an investment. With solid topics of focus and rigorous reflection as part of the process, lab classrooms are indeed a worthy investment in the professional growth of teachers. As is the case with any structure, principals must remain prudent in who they ask to host lab classrooms and the frequency in which they devote precious instructional time to the endeavor.

Occasionally, teachers will ruminate on ideas that are more complex than just deciding to implement an intriguing instructional strategy. On these occasions, teachers contemplate and develop their own theories of learning based on their classroom experiences and wish to test them out with some guidance. In these moments, principals should promote the concept of mini-action research projects for teachers. While these ideas are not necessarily conducted in a format and setting as controlled as one that passes the rigors of a true experimental design, there is a place for teachers to design new practices around a controlled research project.

Many leaders will periodically allow this to take the place of undergoing the formal scrutiny of a typical performance evaluation. This can be a great incentive for teachers to consider the idea but leaders need to maintain a level of quality control and not just go through the motions of treating any idea as the basis for a strong action research project. Likewise, teachers often incorporate these types of projects as the basis for meeting coursework requirements for advanced degrees. This should be embraced as long as it is accompanied by a genuine desire and attempt to understand the classroom instruction in a deeper way.

Action research projects can take many forms and focus on an incredibly wide variety of topics. The best place for a teacher to begin in this regard is to examine a theory that seems to have taken hold within the setting and urge that teacher to test the veracity of the claim. For example, teachers often have widely diverging opinions on the value of homework for secondary students. Some would argue that it is essential to build and reinforce the skills that are learned in the classroom and that students simply cannot get enough practice if they are limited to the minutes within the instructional day. Consider the following scenario as a principal attempts to lead a teacher to entertain the prospect of conducting mini-action research:

Teacher: "I'm still stuck on this problem of homework for my students."

Principal: "It's not going any better since we last talked?"

Teacher: "No, it is just so frustrating. Some kids always do it just because I ask them. Some students will never do it despite my pleading."

Principal: "Does there seem to be a relationship between whether they do their homework and their grade?"

Teacher: "I have always said so. You know, it makes sense. You get better at what you practice, right? But then I have some students who just blow my theory out of the water."

Principal: "How so?"

Teacher: "Well, some students never, I mean never, do my assigned homework and do really well on quizzes and tests. I feel bad because they know more math than any of my other students but their grade doesn't show it."

Principal: "Do you have others on the opposite side of things too?"

Teacher: "Yes! It is maddening. Kids will do every single homework problem and still bomb my quizzes. I feel bad for them because they do what I say it takes to be successful and it just isn't enough."

Principal: "Do you have any ideas going forward?"

Teacher: "I'm not sure what to do. I'm certainly taking suggestions if you have any."

Principal: "Well, I'm not sure I have any solutions at this point, but I think it may be too early to come to a conclusion anyway. Are you interested in conducting a little experiment?"

Teacher: "That depends, I suppose!"

Principal: "Well, I have been wondering about this issue myself and I have a theory I have been working on that I think we could test without adding too much work for you. Do you have sets of homework problems broken down by topic?"

Teacher: "Sure, that isn't an issue. What do you have in mind?"

Principal: "What if students refuse to do your problems because they think they know how to do the problems already and resent the fact that you make them practice things they've already mastered?"

Teacher: "Yeah, some of my kids say as much. Based on their quiz scores, they might be right. But a lot more of them say it than actually do well on quizzes."

Principal: "Right. So, let's call their bluff. Could you tie a set number of problems to each question on a pretest? Then, based on the questions they get wrong, you would only require them to do those sets of problems?"

Teacher: "Yeah, I have heard of that. I think Ms. Rogers does something like that, but I have never tried it."

Principal: "Well, instead of just trying it, let's implement it for a set period of time and track to see if students' grades and willingness to do their homework increases, decreases, or stays the same during the designated period."

Teacher: "Right. I could have the kids graph their weekly progress to increase their buy-in. Maybe I could also have a method for the kids who do the problems already too. I could suggest that they need to complete three problems correctly without outside help before moving on to another type of problem to make sure they really understand rather than just complying with the set number of problems I assign."

Principal: "I like it. If homework is necessary to supply needed practice, let's design a little experiment to see what kind of results we get."

Teacher: "What if it doesn't work though?"

Principal: "Then we know more! Quite honestly, while I have my suspicions, I don't really know what we might find. That's why we should do the experiment."

The principal in this scenario is confronted by a teacher who is clearly frustrated. The teacher desires to do the right thing but is beginning to question historical practices in a way that is making it difficult to proceed in a sensible way. Sometimes, teachers get a bit lost. The principal begins by reacquainting themself with the problem the teacher has previously described. Before trying to prematurely supply answers for this teacher, the principal asks a number of clarifying questions to try to bring the issue to a head in a way that some experimentation may support.

In fact, the principal acknowledges that there is uncertainty in the outcome of the suggested idea. The focus is on seeking out answers rather than suggesting beforehand what ought to be done. This is in keeping with the spirit of true experimentation. While the scientist may have a hypothesis beforehand, the point of the experiment is to find answers that provide insight to the researcher rather than filtering observations to fit a predetermined outcome. The principal may be able to offer insight and suggestions on some occasions. However, there is great wisdom in supporting a teacher through work that has no obvious answer. The role that mini-action research can provide in these times keeps teachers from falling into a sense of hopelessness and frustration and can keep teachers focused on new angles to their work when the answers aren't easy to find.

Each of the structures described in this chapter provides a type of arrangement within the school system that can grow and move teachers in their work. Education has moved past a point where educators can operate in isolation from each other. The demands of education and the needs of students are simply too great for teachers to work by themselves. Working as a unit focused on a common goal is often easier said than done, however.

Leaders must recognize that there is more to collaboration and professional development than what is historically considered. Providing a time and space for adults to work together is certainly a good start. True leadership demands that the leader remain involved in the creation and support of collaborative structures to ensure that teachers are not spinning their wheels in contrived meetings that serve very little purpose. Left on their own, teachers will spend their time collaborating in ways they see fit. This may not always match with the best use of very limited noninstructional hours within a school day.

Principals must exercise just enough control and participation of these collaborative structures to maintain a level of consistency and authenticity to their designed purpose. Each of these structures has a definite and established purpose. It is likely that teachers will embrace each of them in a different way depending upon the topic and level of comfort they have with the proposed plan. Leaders should remain very tight on their insistence for all teachers to participate within their collaborative team. This work should never be seen as optional, and the principal should retain firm control of the topics that should be discussed. The principal should loosen up on the ideas that are produced within those tightly controlled obligations. The teachers should retain their strong voices and opinions on what to do next for students. They should not be allowed to use those strong voices to decide whether they need to meet. Likewise, leaders should be very insistent that all teachers be a part of instructional rounds within the building.

Keeping everyone involved in the process without giving some the opportunity to opt out supports a culture of collaboration within the building and forces teachers to consider how others approach their work. Likely, teachers have developed opinions about their peers. This work ensures that those opinions are fair and well informed based on personal observations. Leaders should organize lab classrooms in a way that involves everybody, but the selection of these teams should not be random.

This structure demands forethought in putting together a small cohort of teachers who will engage in the process but the conversational dynamic that is required demands that a leader put these teams together thoughtfully. The presence of the principal in these lab classrooms is essential to ensure that the process is healthy and that the hosts feel comfortable as they open up their practice to the scrutiny of others. However, it is also important to create a good mix of personalities to encourage an environment that is lively and productive.

Principals must keep a steady hand on leading these collaborative structures as they can fall apart in an instant. Because this work is focused on bringing professionals together in their work, it brings with it the weaknesses and insecurities of the people involved. It is not easy for teachers to sit in an environment where they recognize that those around them may have more insight or greater skill as a professional. In these moments, it is easy for teachers to react poorly or even shut down entirely. The only way for a principal to manage these complex social interactions is by keeping the focus of the work in its proper place.

From start to finish, principals must focus this work on the prospect that everyone can do better. The principal cannot allow some teachers to develop a cult of personality because they are seen as experts in ways that their peers are not. Likewise, the principal must safeguard against teachers who take part in these structures and leave in a worse place than when they began the work. The only way that this is possible to maintain is to require personal reflection from all members that values the demand that everyone must grow in their practice.

Above all else, leaders must keep the focus of all of these proposed structures on the students. As accomplished as any teacher may be, there are always students who are lagging behind in a given classroom. There is always at least one student who is not achieving in the same ways as their peers. Seen in this light, even superstar teachers have a long way to go in their journey and cannot rightfully claim that they have already arrived. As such, principals should demand that student work be an essential part of every collaborative conversation. If teachers have decided to use a new instructional protocol, they must be required to show completed student work using it. If teachers decide to implement a new strategy for reviewing student work because of instructional rounds, they must bring it to their next meeting. If the participants of a lab classroom determine that they do not intend to use the strategies showcased by the lab host, they must bring completed student work to show what they are doing instead.

In this work, it is always appropriate to disagree or suggest alternatives, but teachers must bring student work with them to demonstrate the fruits of that instructional choice. Student work keeps everyone honest in the conversation. Student work buttresses strong philosophical opinions. Student work is a great leveling force to ensure that the best ideas are the ones that are implemented for students.

Chapter 9

Living in the Trenches

There is no turning back. Once a principal has made the decision to become fundamentally intertwined in the very fabric of instruction in a school, nothing will ever be the same. To begin in this work forces teachers to see a leader in a new light. When old ways are cast off and new actions become part of daily operation, teachers quickly forget previous times when the principal was disconnected from the true work of teachers.

Teachers who have experienced a true instructional leader have a hard time returning to any other way. A principal may have once been able to skirt the question, "Why don't you come into my classroom more?" As tough as that question may be to answer, there is a much more difficult one that a principal may face that is only altered by one tiny but significant word, "Why don't you come into my class *anymore*?" How might a well-meaning principal answer the question without an accompanying sense of dread and disappointment that so much progress and potential has slipped away?

This work demands a profound reordering of priorities for a school administrator. In many ways, former practices have to be set aside and new ones must come to exist in their place. Trying to reconcile both a managerial approach and a leadership approach to running the building becomes nearly impossible. Certainly, some tasks need to be managed, but people need a leader. Principals should note that there are stages of implementation in transforming their leadership into a more intimate relationship with classroom instruction. For many principals, easing into the suggested practices is absolutely appropriate. Gaining ground with each classroom visit is a noble way to proceed. Leaders must begin by occupying easily taken territory. There are many teachers who are receptive to the very work that the principal is trying to improve. Leaders must methodically make strides by investing in person after person with every possible conversation.

Principals should not make the mistake in thinking this work is simply about their presence. While being present is certainly a prerequisite to becoming involved in the work that is happening in the instructional trenches, it will never be sufficient. To be present without becoming involved is to be a bystander in the most important work. Teachers may actually resent a leader more if they are near the work but unable or unwilling to play a role than if the principal were completely absent. Finding a voice to accompany a presence in the instructional setting takes time and practice. The only way to strengthen this voice is by repeated efforts to become more relevant in a teacher's professional life. Principals should be reassured, however, that most teachers will immediately appreciate a leader's efforts in implementing these changes. Evolving as a professional by adopting new practices is not easy, and teachers will be supportive of efforts that show the leader values their work and seeks to understand it better.

If principals choose to adapt their practices in ways that support teachers in their work, they will need to make some difficult decisions in what kind of work will no longer fit into the daily routine of the principal because new practices and structures are now valued instead. Thus far, the list of recommended practices includes having increased presence in classrooms through firsthand observations, engaging teachers in deep conversations about what is happening in their classrooms, ensuring a presence in collaborative team meetings, implementing routine instructional rounds, instituting lab classrooms, and supporting mini-action research projects. Each of these proposed structures demands a commitment to both time and energy on the part of the principal to ensure that they function as intended.

In the beginning of this work, principals began by committing a block of their daily calendar to visiting classrooms. With the addition of these new structures, principals must formally plan how to incorporate each of them into the academic calendar. School calendars have a rhythm to them, and planning for any event must be deliberate in light of the demands of each month. For example, leaders should front-load a lot of their time in classroom observations in the beginning of the year as school gets started. This will set a strong tone for the year and will get both students and teachers accustomed to the presence of the principal in classrooms focused on instruction. Trying to pull teachers out of their classrooms to host a lab classroom in the beginning of the year when teachers are trying to establish good habits and procedures for their students would be a mistake.

In contrast, many of the other structures are situational and can be implemented when an occasion presents itself, and a leader should remain vigilant for opportunities to support new work. Leaders should also recognize that this work should be thoughtfully spread out through a year in a way that does not risk burning teachers out.

A final aspect of the principal's planning for new work should be a systematic attempt to groom new teacher leaders. If leaders seek to develop teacher leaders, this cannot be left purely to circumstances and obvious opportunities. If a leader blocks off time in the calendar to observe classrooms and lead instructional rounds, that leader should also block off a specific period of time at regular intervals to develop teacher leaders. Using this designated time to invest in teachers with the specific purpose of increasing their leadership capacity is the only way to guarantee that this work will take root and not be left to chance.

Principals may rightly wonder when all of these new instructional duties can actually happen within the busy schedule of a modern building administrator. Leaders must constantly review their calendars and daily planners to ensure that they are fiercely protective of these commitments. Principals may have to forgo some of their historically important daily activities before engaging in this new work. With the exception of supporting collaborative team meetings, most of this work must happen during instructional time within a school day. Principals should audit their calendar to see if some of the work they do throughout the day is actually happening at the wrong time. For example, principals are often forced to complete extensive paperwork for district and state reports, improvement plans, and discipline logs. This paperwork is certainly necessary and an integral part of a principal's job. However, there is no reason that this paperwork must be completed when class is in session.

Readjusting the order in which principals tackle each of their commitments can often free up considerable blocks of time to support instruction in classrooms. Being willing to swap commitments is part of the approach a principal must take if the many obligations of a principal are to be met. However, principals may also find that some of the items that were formerly clogging the calendar such as discipline events and teachers seeking an audience with the principal are actually diminished because of the associated increase in visibility and access that teachers and students have to their instructional leader.

Of course, a principal must find a balance in all of this work. How much is enough? The work described thus far may give the impression that principals should be constantly present in the instructional lives of teachers. Although most principals have strayed so far from having a classroom presence that a strong commitment to be present is in order, principals must seek an optimal amount of support for teachers. More is not always better. Maintaining a constantly evolving presence and withdrawal from the instructional environment is an art form in itself.

Principals must remember that they are the supervisors of teachers. Teachers never forget that the principal is their boss. As deep and collegial as the professional conversation may be between a teacher and principal, a formal power structure looms in the background and cannot be denied. Principals may not have any interest in flexing their professional muscle as they go about their day-to-day business. This does not, however, mean that teachers do not constantly look at their principal as their superior.

Principals must realize that it is not as easy as reassuring teachers that they do not need to think about their boss as their superior when they engage in instructional conversations. While this fact does not prevent conversations from happening, a principal's presence does indeed alter the conversation. The conversations between teachers are *always* different in the presence of an administrator. This is not to suggest that conversations are less honest or are contrived because a principal is present. However, the conversation is always altered because of a principal's presence.

Likewise, this does not mean that the conversation is necessarily better or worse because the principal is a part of it. On some occasions, the presence of a school leader may shape the conversation into a better place. Principals exercising strong and appropriate leadership skills with teachers can initiate and sustain instructional conversations that may not exist without the principal playing a role. Conversely, the presence of a principal in a conversation may occasionally stunt the natural conversation.

When anyone is in the presence of their superior, there may be a natural tendency to edit and adapt the things that are said because the leader is listening. Principals have to ask themselves some hard questions in these moments. When is it appropriate for the principal to be purposefully absent? School leaders often gloss over these awkward moments by urging teachers to speak freely assuring the teachers that there will not be any repercussions for giving an unedited viewpoint. Principals need to ask themselves whether this is entirely true. Often, principals will have the self-control to allow an unpopular comment to be made after urging faculty members to speak freely. However, principals remember things that are said. If a teacher is taking an unacceptable stance on an issue but happens to be swayed over in time, a principal needs to reflect deeply on how that moment will be remembered.

Principals often secretly harbor resentment that lingers when teachers don't immediately come on board to their preferred way of thinking. In these moments, might a principal be reluctant to ask for that teacher's opinion on other significant matters because of the way the teacher chose to speak out when they were encouraged to do so without fearing any consequences? The price that teachers pay for speaking up when they were told it was safe to do so is not always immediate. Teachers have felt the distance and coldness from principals who have claimed to embrace a free exchange of opinions when that was only the superficial truth of the matter.

Principals do not need to look any further than their own relationship with their superior to assess whether their offer is realistic. Principals do not always speak openly and freely with their superiors even when urged to do so. Just as principals have reservations in this way, they need to respect that their urging for teachers to be honest with them might be edited to varying degrees depending upon the teacher. Since this can be the reality of conversations as a principal develops deeper levels of trust with faculty members, it is important for the principal to recognize that there are certain times when the principal should simply stay away.

Asking a principal to stay away from important instructional conversations may seem counterintuitive to the advice of being present in more frequent and deeper ways. However, principals should recognize that retreating in a battle may assist in winning the eventual war. Choosing to be absent should be as conscious of a decision as being immersed in instructional work. In the moments where principals recognize that they should allow a conversation to occur and evolve without their participation, leaders should thoughtfully plan how and when they will rejoin the work and get up to speed.

Seen in this light, the principal is acting much like the parent who sometimes retreats to allow the child to walk a few steps without their hand being held. The parent remains tuned in to the needs of the child and is vigilant in the need to reengage at any moment, but they are is also cognizant that some steps have to be taken alone in the natural maturation of the child. Teachers are certainly not toddlers with respect to their skills and abilities, but whether their hand needs to be held or whether they need to take a few steps alone is an apt parallel in the way teachers working together need to mature as professionals.

Sometimes, the most exciting and compelling conversations are the very ones from which principals must excuse themselves. This can be very difficult for a principal who desperately wants to be a part of engaging work. Leaders have a constant urge to lead. In these moments, principals must exercise personal restraint to preserve the greater good at the expense of their own professional curiosity and interest. Leadership, at times, involves allowing others to walk out in front while the leader recedes into the background until their presence is, once again, most needed.

There will be times when teachers will seek out principals and enlist them to join in especially difficult conversations. Of course, principals desire to help others and can often get sucked into the problems of others when teachers approach them in this way. The problems that teachers bring to the principal are often very real. For their part, principals often shift immediately into problem-solving mode and become immersed in how they can help resolve problems between groups of teachers. Before taking on the problems of others as their own, principals must first stop and examine the true nature of what is happening when teachers are in conflict and seek the principal to intervene.

At times, the difficulties are real and demand the impartial involvement of the principal to bring peace to those in crisis. However, teachers may also bring principals into problems that may not be appropriate for the principal to address. When problems are brought to an administrator, the leaders should listen very carefully to the issue that has been brought forward. After fully understanding the issue, principals should first determine who should be the person to address the problem.

For example, if a teacher is frustrated with a colleague for borrowing supplies without returning them in good order, they may bring their complaint immediately to the principal. Certainly, the principal could visit with the other teacher and ask them to be more cordial in the way they share materials. However, principals must first ask themselves whether this is really the type of problem that they should personally address. Often, teachers will enlist the principal in assisting with problems that arise because difficult conversations are easier to bring to a third party than to address personally.

Most people do not relish having to address and resolve conflict and are content to allow someone else to smooth things out for them. This, pattern, however, can easily be misused. Principals should not allow themselves to become the solution for others when they are easily capable of doing it themselves. Principals should not fix problems simply because they can. This undermines the need for professionals to find their own voice in the professional conversation and often strips away the very leadership abilities that the principal seeks to build within others.

Principals must remain vigilant that they do not engage inappropriately in choosing sides as work evolves in a building and divisions begin to emerge. Teachers who believe strongly in their work are likely to seek the approval of their superior. While this may seem natural, it can easily pit principals against other teachers in a way where sides are drawn up prematurely.

When tensions arise between teachers, sometimes allowing them to work through the difficulties that emerge is part of a healthy process of teamwork and collaboration. Many decades ago, when ecologists began growing trees in the Biosphere 2 project, they noticed that the trees they were growing in their self-contained indoor ecosystem struggled to thrive. These trees never quite reached maturity and lacked the strength to stand up completely on their own. The scientists underestimated the role that wind played in strengthening a plant to make it healthy and vibrant.

It is easy to assume that protecting a tree from the damage that the wind can inflict would be a good thing and be one less variable that scientists would have to consider. The truth was quite the contrary. The stress that the wind brings to a plant helps make it stronger and more able to withstand its own weight. Those trees eventually collapsed upon themselves as a result. The adversity of the wind is needed.

This parallels the healthy stress that teachers must endure to grow and mature within their profession. In the same way that hurricane winds can be too forceful and damage a tree irreparably, unhealthy stress is not good for a person and can be quite detrimental. This should not suggest that teachers should be protected from all stressors in the educational setting. Some of the winds of change and adversity will be the very conditions that provide the resistance that strengthens their character and resolve that will make them grow as they are intended. To shelter teachers from each and every difficulty is to remove them from the very environmental factors they need.

Principals should be mindful of this when they decide whether to insert themselves into a debate. While they may be able to choose sides and bring the conflict to resolution, it may do more harm than good. A true leader manages the tension between groups often allowing those involved to work through difficulties as it hones their professional positions and requires them to collaboratively labor through their work. Short-term thinking may suggest that endorsing the opinion of one group over another is appropriate if the opinion is clearly superior. However, weighing in with the professional sway and influence of a principal's positional power may cause unintended harm in stunting the healthy discourse that comes through resistance. Remaining steady and confident in other people's abilities to work through difficult times is part of a leader's thoughtfulness and prudence.

This is not always easy when a teacher comes to a principal and is clearly in need of help. This is further exacerbated if the principal recognizes that they could easily jump into the conversation and likely bring a swift resolution to the frustration the teacher is experiencing. Instead, the principal should listen closely and determine if the principal should indeed address the problem personally or if the way the leader should solve the problem is by empowering teachers to sharpen their own tools to fix the problem themselves. Because principals are busy and are often viewed as efficient problem solvers, teachers will likely bring problems of every sort to them to address. In the following example, a teacher brings a principal a problem and asks the principal to solve it.

Teacher: "Thanks for seeing me this morning. I know you are very busy."

Principal: "No problem at all. What can I do to help?"

Teacher: "It's my collaborative team. I can't stand it anymore. Do I have to keep working with them?"

Principal: "I assume you mean Mr. Taft and Ms. Ripley?"

Teacher: "Yes, we all teach world history, and they just bully me. I know I'm only a second-year teacher, but I don't think they should get to boss me around like they do."

Principal: "When you say they boss you around, what do you mean by that?"

Teacher: "When we meet each morning, all we ever do is listen to what they have done as a lesson for the past ten years and then they shame me if I won't just take their lessons and materials and copy what they do."

Principal: "How do they respond if you suggest approaching things in a different way?"

Teacher: "Well, they don't actually say I can't do what I want, but they just make me feel like I should be doing what they say and I'm doing things wrong."

Principal: "Please keep in mind that they are your team, but I am your evaluator. I will let you know if I see you engaging in inferior instructional practices. In fact, I've been in on a few occasions and told you quite the opposite, right?"

Teacher: "Yes, you've been supportive of me, but I just don't like meeting with them."

Principal: "I can understand that it can be frustrating. Have you talked to them about your frustration either as a group or separately?"

Teacher: "I usually just act like I will do what they say and then just do my own thing, but I know it bothers them. Should I just do it their way?"

Principal: "No. Your ideas bring a fresh perspective to that group. But I wouldn't suggest that you pretend you will use their materials either. You need to find your voice in the group. Do you think you can talk to them about your ideas?"

Teacher: "I think they'd bite my head off if I disagree with their methods."

Principal: "But you don't have to comment on their methods at all. It is not an either/or proposition. Do you think you can tell them that you appreciate that they share their work, but then explain what you intend to do?"

Teacher: "I don't think I'll convince them to see it may way."

Principal: "That's just it, though. You don't have to convince them to do it your way. You simply need to offer ideas that you believe are valid and explain why. The first step is to just find your voice by explaining your approach. You don't have to convince them of anything. In fact, ask what their opinion may be of your idea. Even if they are critical, at least you've begun to discuss more than just their ideas in the group, right?"

Teacher: "I can try. I'm not very hopeful that it will go well though."

Principal: "You really have nothing to lose, but everything to gain. You do not have to change your approach based on anything they say, but I do believe they will begin considering your opinion in a new way even if they disagree. Right now, it is about getting your voice in the room. I cannot be your voice. I have all the faith in the world you can do this. Your ideas are good ones, and they will stand on their own merits."

The principal in this scenario is faced with a teacher who is on the verge of shutting down professionally within the collaborative team and is looking for the principal to come to the rescue. Certainly, the principal could have stepped in and demanded that everyone listen to the young teacher, but that would have been a mistake. While the other teachers may be overbearing and pushy, they had not really done anything wrong that demanded that they be reprimanded.

The root of the problem, as the principal discovered, was that the teacher had good ideas but no voice within the team. When the principal first suggested that the teacher needed to advocate for himself rather than the principal, the teacher once again wanted to shut down by offering objections that the group could not possibly be convinced. Again, the principal remained steady in the conversation noting that the purpose of the work is not always to convince. The teacher had framed the solution in the wrong way. The first step was to find the courage to put a voice in the room. Seen in that light, the teacher was at least willing to try. Of course, the principal recognized that the first attempt would not likely radically transform the team dynamic, but it would likely shift the tone enough to allow the teacher some genuine space at the table.

One technique a principal can use after listening to a teacher's concerns is to ask, "What is it exactly that you'd like me to do?" Although this may seem obvious, many leaders do not always venture past trying to understand the problem that is being described. When principals ask this question, it forces the teachers to consider what they are, in fact, asking to be done. When teachers are unsure how to answer, a principal can inquire whether the teacher just needed to vent a little, or if they are looking for some advice, or if the teacher is actually requesting that the principal intervene in some way. Often, teachers begin an emotional conversation believing that they need the principal to become the solution for them, but through a supportive conversation, they realize that they themselves can resolve their problems afterward.

Principals can create a culture of positivity and support through every interaction within the school setting if strong norms are established to define professional behavior. While the practice of setting norms certainly has merits, it cannot be a superficial set of rules governing behavior. For example, schools may have norms about the importance of being on time and putting electronic devices on silent mode during meetings. These practices may be necessary, but they only hint at the true reason why norms need to be set.

Principals should frame group norms around one simple question, "How will we agree to treat each other on the day we disagree completely?" This question gets to the heart of the reason why norms are necessary in the first place. Adults often disagree and their ability to remain professional becomes strained. In daily interactions, teachers are unlikely to need norms to guide their behavior. However, in the moments where teachers passionately and fundamentally disagree with one another, they may need to fall back on the promises they made to each other. Establishing these promises in a moment when they aren't upset with each other protects them in vulnerable moments when emotions begin to run high.

Reaffirming how professionals treat each other and their students when they are frustrated and angry is essential for a principal to keep the landscape of the school safe, positive, and healthy. Only in this sort of environment are teachers likely to grow and flourish in their profession. Without this firm grasp on the way people treat each other, no instructional structure conceived can produce an environment where both teachers and students excel.

Functioning as a principal in the challenging world that is public education is no easy task. Aside from the countless crises and urgent demands that are placed upon educators, principals are challenged to emerge as true instructional leaders of their schools. Developing strong systems to manage pockets of emerging leadership and healthy practice takes thoughtfulness and planning on the part of the school leader. In addition to careful structuring and planning to grow teachers in their profession, principals cannot always predict when an opportunity to support new work may present itself.

Principals must hone the complementary skills of being organized and structured in the way they promote great instructional practices and yet nimble and on the lookout for emerging opportunities. This cannot happen if a principal only views the job as keeping a lid on problems that may erupt within the school. Problems do indeed emerge, but they cannot take the focus away from the true purpose of schools.

One way principals can increase the likelihood of creating a dynamic learning environment is to make a commitment to say "yes" to ideas with potential. It is easy to find reasons to say no to an idea or request. Principals often cite limited resources or potential policy entanglements as reasons to shut down new thinking. Although every idea may not be a good one, many suspect ideas could be revamped into decent ones with a little bit of thought and consideration. There are sufficient problems within public education that a principal should take great pause before deciding against a new idea that may help students. Public education needs more possible solutions.

Trying to be supportive of the myriad ideas that may bubble up can be quite taxing in itself. However, if principals are trying to light a fire under both teachers and students in their school, they need to be willing to encourage the random grass fires of great practice that unpredictably catch in schools. Small grass fires are often the cause of uncontrollable blazes spreading across great expanses requiring very little encouragement. So too are the grass fires of great instruction. These isolated and small efforts can often penetrate silos of closed thinking and practice in transformative ways. In these moments, principals simply need to offer the small bit of support and encouragement that great people need and only need to intervene if the work departs from the underlying mission and vision of the school. These efforts will likely bring more substantive change than any mandated practices that come from the top down.

In education, educators often justify both good and suspect practices by invoking the well-worn sentiment that "we do what's best for kids." On occasion, this statement does indeed preserve practices that serve students well and ensure their success. However, this is not always the case. It is just as likely to be said as a polite rejection to new or innovate practices that may stretch what teachers are willing to do. Perhaps the best way to transform this conversation is by reframing that comment by asking, "What should we do *next* for kids?" This is the guiding principle for all educators.

The fate of our students is inextricably bound up within the actions of our leaders. Many suggest that educators must remain patient in this work. However, that depends largely on how one defines the word patience. For some, it is defined as the capacity to tolerate delay. By this definition, patience is unacceptable in the critical work that must be done for our children. The Latin root word for patience is *patientia*, meaning to "suffer with." To suffer with someone is to join in their struggles and frustrations as they come to a better place. In this sense, leaders must exercise great patience. Principals must lead by suffering with both teachers and students as they struggle to find their way. To accept delay, however, is no longer an option.

About the Author

Dr. Stephen V. Newton has worked as a teacher, school administrator, and academic professional at the K–12, college, and university levels for over twenty-four years. He currently serves as the director of curriculum and instruction for the local school district in Cheyenne, Wyoming. He also serves an educational consultant focused on leadership development, data analysis, postsecondary readiness, and literacy. Stephen is married to Amanda, an attorney, and has been blessed with six wonderful children.